Thank You
Introduction
Quotation
Foreword
Part I.
"The Floor" 19
Chapter 1 20
"Come back tomorrow and you can start" 20
Chapter 2 25
"The Floor" 25
Chapter 3 29
"And They're Off!" 29
Chapter 4 34
"My First Day Ends" 34
Chapter 5 39
"We're going where?" 39
Chapter 6 44
"Vegas" 44
Chapter 7 51
"Attention" 51
Chapter 8 59
"Promotion and Out-trades" 59
Chapter 9 66
"On My Own" 66
Chapter 10 70
"Cocaine" 70
Chapter 11 77
"I Quit" 77
Chapter 12 85
"Two Steps Backward" 85
Chapter 13 90
"I'm Back" 90
Chapter 14 93
"The New Floor" 93
Chapter 15 98
"Shannon's Wave" 98
Chapter 16 103

"Bob"	103
Chapter 17	108
"ING"	108
Chapter 18	114
"Trading"	114
Chapter 19	126
"Rage"	126
Chapter 20	132
"Filling the Black Hole"	132
Chapter 21	137
"Dodging Bullets"	137
Chapter 22	141
"Changes"	141
Chapter 23	144
"The Black Hole Widens"	144
Part II	148
"The Second Pit"	148
Chapter 24	149
"Shame"	149
Chapter 25	151
"Confusion"	151
Chapter 26	155
"Leaping Into a New Pit"	155
Chapter 27	166
"Change"	166
Chapter 28	169
"Group"	169
Chapter 29	173
"Marriage and the Ashes"	173
Chapter 30	179
"Letting Go"	179
Chapter 31	185
"Affective Work"	185
Chapter 32	190
"Rob and the Onion"	190
Chapter 33	196
"The Opportunity"	196

Chapter 34	201
"Practice, Practice, Practice"	201
Chapter 35	206
"The Only Way Through It is Through It"	206
Chapter 36	210
"Turning Point"	210
Chapter 37	213
"Life without liquor"	213
Chapter 38	233
"Men"	233
Chapter 39	240
"Career Death and Projection"	240
Chapter 40	247
"Cutting the Cord"	247
Chapter 41	252
"Staying the Course"	252
Chapter 42	255
"Jung"	255
Chapter 43	261
"Leaving Mom's Teepee"	261
Chapter 44	267
"My Father"	267
Chapter 45	272
"September 7th 1995"	272
Chapter 46	273
"Conclusion"	273
Afterword	275
Self-Help Resources	279
Quotes	280
About the Author	283

Copyright Information

All rights reserved.
Copyright© James A. Goulding and James A. Goulding Coach Works, Inc.
Lombard and Elmhurst Illinois.
This book may not be reproduced or transmitted in any form or by any means electronic or mechanical, including photocopying, recording, or by any information storage and retrieval system, without permission in writing from the Author, James A. Goulding.

ISBN number-0-9717606-0-8

"Printed in the U.S.A by RJ Communications"
Please visit RJ Communications at
www.booksjustbooks.com
Or write them at 51 East 42 St. Ste. 1202
New York, New York 10017

First printing 1000 copies
This book is self published by James A. Goulding and James A. Goulding Coach Works, Inc.

For ordering information, wholesale or retail please call or email;
James A. Goulding
708-774-9321
jamesg4@yahoo.com

Ms. Angela Grigsby edited, "Part I" of this book.

The entire book was re-edited by Randy Littlejohn.
P.O. Box 563
Oakhurst, CA 93644-0563

Cover Design by
Jonathan Gullery
HSA DESIGN
4 West 43rd Street
New York, New York 10036
PH. 212.575.5091 FX. 212.819.1999
Email; jg@midcity.net

THANK YOU

I would like to thank the following people for whom this book would never have been written. They say it takes a community to raise someone. These people are from my community.

Randy Littlejohn, editor of this book. Randy took a book that was written in a stream-of-conscious style and made it concise and to the point. How lucky I am to have found such a talented editor. The relationship between editor and writer is a difficult one, from the editor's point of view. The writer is emotionally involved in the work and the editor isn't. The editor must tread lightly as not to offend the writer. Randy is a master at this. Furthermore, it is my feeling that half of the credit of authoring this book should have gone to Randy. The cover should read, by Jim Goulding with Randy Littlejohn. Bless you Randy for believing in my book.

Jonathan Gullery. My Graphics designer. What a fantastic job you did on the cover! I'm very lucky to have found you.

Booksjustbooks.com. (RJ Communications). Did we print a great book or what!

Diana Goulding. My soul mate, friend and wife of 18 years who has been there from the beginning. I am the luckiest person on the earth to have met you.

Haley Dara Goulding. My daughter, who teaches me to live in the moment, every day. I love you with all my heart and soul.

Jay M., you have no idea how much you did for me. Maybe it's time to tell you. "Thank you Jay."

Bob Laser. Who mentored and guided me while I was young and naïve. He was personally responsible for a great deal of my success at the Chicago Board of Trade. I will forever be thankful for the years I spent in the Bond pit, working with Bob.

The Chicago Board of Trade. An institution that I believe stands for capitalism. The type of capitalism that this Nation was founded on. An institution that allows a 17-year-old to enter its' doors and build a career.

Doug Erdmier. For teaching me how to conduct business as a gentlemen.

Bill Erdmier and Branko Boricich. For bringing me back.

All of my customers at the Chicago Board of Trade and the people who worked on the floor for them. Without a doubt I couldn't have been successful if you didn't believe in me.

Mark and Andy. If not for the both of you, I'd have gone nowhere. Thanks for your constant and unwavering support.

Tim Anderson who mentored me while on this Earth.

Jerry Maloney. Thank you for mentoring me while I was still a teenager and carrying so much responsibility at Refco.

Tom Dittmer for taking a chance on a 17-year-old.

Jerry Keeley and Dan Conrad who kept me sane.

Each and every one of the employees who worked for me. With out you I couldn't have succeeded.

Jim Corbeil. I never could be your boss, because you are my friend.

Brian Porter and Larry Friedman who kept me laughing in the pit.

Dan Brennan, for being my life long friend and guiding me to the right decision.

John Large and Ed Reda. Thank you for guiding me in the complicated world of accounting and Law. How lucky am I to have found an accountant and a lawyer who are both honest and full of integrity, not to mention, dedicated family men.

Rob Ahrens, Judith Palmer, Jane Siepel, Dave Lingren, Karen Kobzan, Paul Guistolise, and Clarice Sinars. If not for each of you, I'd be dead. You knew the battle I faced. You led me the whole way. May your God bless each and every one of you. Rest in peace Karen.

Nanci Greene. The greatest piano teacher on this Planet. The greatest listener and someone who I call a dear friend.

The first Thursday night group, thank you for the container.

The second Thursday night group, thank you for letting me be me.

All my brothers from the Man Kind Project. Whoa. Unbelievable. Outstanding. Fantastic. You all touched me and I am very lucky I crossed paths with each and every one of you.

Ellen & Ed Rose, for taking the time to read the first rough draft of the book. For being great friends and great neighbors. You witnessed the transformation first hand and supported me all the way. Bless you both.

John Savel and Dave Duerkop. For taking the time to read the second draft of this book and giving me there honest opinions, which I hold dear.

Renee Mitchell for reading the third draft of this book. Offering her insights and also for being a wonderful friend.

My grandfather, Peter Goulding Sr., for taking the journey.

My great-grandfather, Maurice Murphy, for taking the journey.

My Brother Bill, My sisters, Aileen, Barb and Maureen. The bond we all share between us is nothing less than extraordinary. (I miss Reg.)

My sister Regina who suddenly passed away while I was writing this book. I'll miss you more than you'll ever know. Rest in peace.

And last, but certainly not least, my parents, Mary and Peter who never lost faith.

Introduction

By Jim Goulding

Writing has always come naturally to me and I knew I'd produce a book sooner or later. I just needed to sober up! Never in a million years did I think my first book would be a Memoir. I'm too young to be writing a Memoir; I'm only 39. However, in the sixteen-years this book covers, I lived a lifetime.

"From the Pits to the Pits", is written in two parts. The first part begins In September 1979 when I was 17-years-old. I enter the Chicago Board of Trade (CBOT) as a runner and begin to build a career there. This is the first pit. I chronicle my rise from a runner to a million dollar broker. I'll take you directly to the trading floor and the inner world of the CBOT. You'll enter the chaos of the trading pits and come to understand what it's all about.

You'll run with me through my meteoric rise and fall. Along the way I'll tell inside stories about other traders and the fortunes they made and lost. You'll stumble with me as I succumb to the pressures of success and inner demons. Finally, you'll follow me into the world of drugs and alcohol.

The first part of the book concludes in October of 1988 as I hit bottom.

"Part II", starts in October of 1988 as we enter a second pit filled with my own demons. As I try to recover from severe drug and alcohol abuse we journey into the world of intensive psychotherapy. You'll meet the people who saved my life and helped me tame the demons. Slowly I begin to put the pieces of my life together, including the reconciliation of my marriage. Then I face the final demon. Part II ends in September 1995 when I leave the CBOT for good and am fully recovered from my addictions.

Although this is a story of incredible success and failure and rebirth, it is also and most importantly a book about the search for a relationship with my father. It's a quest for my father's hallowed attention and approval and the devastating effects this quest had on me.

I know that there are many people out there who feel just like I have, who feel alone and desperate. Although this is a Memoir, my sincere hope is that two things will happen as you read my book. Many of you will connect with the underlying themes. Some of you may relate to the relationships I had with my family and co-workers or maybe to my drug and alcohol recovery. I offer you tangible tips and inspiration. In the back of the book you'll see a section for places you can begin your recovery. Or if you just want someone to talk to, you'll see listings for help finding a therapist. Secondly, I hope that you will hear a message loud and clear: reach out and ask for help. Know that you are not alone. Know that family relationships can be repaired. Know that you too can live without drugs, alcohol or any other addiction. If my book gives you hope, and I think it will, then I have succeeded.

Feel free to email me anytime. I will answer you. You can find my information and other information about me in the 'Afterword'. Take care and enjoy.
-Jim
March 2001 to November 2001.

QUOTATIONS

I have been passionate about music since I was a little boy. Music permeates my soul and thankfully doesn't let go. It has lifted me from the darkest corners of depression and enhanced the good times as well.

Although I can play some rhythm guitar badly and Beethoven, Chopin and some Mozart on the piano pretty well, my true gift is the joy of listening.

Two rock bands have deeply influenced my life. Throughout "Part I" of the book you'll read quotes at the beginning of each chapter by these masterminds.

I'd like to thank Pink Floyd and Rush for their gifts of music. I have listened to both bands since I was in grade school and continue to listen today. ('Animals' is playing as I write this and I just listened to 'Counterparts'!) I cannot put into words the magic both bands have brought me, both in concert and at home. (You know you're a Rush fan when you name your cat Geddy Lee!)

From album to eight track to cassette to CD to Video and now DVD, their sounds and stories never get old.

The music they play is nothing less than spectacular. Both the lyrics and the instruments carry a message. In this book I will include the lyrics of Pink Floyds' Roger Waters and Rushs' Neil Peart. Both men are simply genius. I encourage you to listen to their music. You'll miss the full story if you don't hear the music.

A special thanks to Peter Lutteman who's web site I used to collect specific information about certain Rush albums.

www.geocities.com/rushweden/discography.htm

Another special thanks to www.pinkfloyd-co.com for their great web site. Their site assisted me in my research on specific album credits. I suggest you visit this great site for tons of great information about Pink Floyd.

Look in the back of this book for more information on both bands and credit for their work.

FOREWORD

Jim Goulding: The Embrace of Life
By Rob Ahrens
Licensed Clinical Social Worker
President, Conscious Health Initiative, Inc.

Writing a Memoir is a fascinating task. It begs the questions: What is the meaning or value of life?, of any life?, of this life?, of my life? What do I embrace as the significance of being awake, attentive to my existence, and responsible for my presence? What are the consequences (results) of my awakening? Are there lessons in and of my life, which transcend my time, and which may enlighten the awakening paths of others? Are my musings more than the petty wonderings of a starving ego unconsciously designed to further clutter the minds of lost and disembodied souls?

To meet, engage, embrace and enjoy the presence of Jim Goulding is to dive into the river of life itself. His passion for conflict, his creativity, his courage, his cleverness, cunning, and common sense, his integrity and intelligence are touchable, palpable and real. His willingness and ability to enter into and transcend the pain and suffering of family crises and separation, social temptations and seductions, economic challenge, success, adversity and loss, and emotional emptiness and enlightenment are an inspiration to the faint of heart. His love and reverence for heartfelt connections to his family and friends offer insights into the clarity and purpose of an awakened being. The humility and grace of this gentle man are balanced by the strength and power of his commitment to know and speak the truth of his convictions: His "walk" matches his "talk".

The life and memoir of Jim Goulding is not the only life or even the best life to live. It is the reflections of one man on the gifts of showing up, paying attention, acting with integrity, and making a difference in the only life he knows—his own. He has some lessons to reveal and release about surrendering to the reality of his existence, accepting and working with his burdens and limitations, forgiving yet not forgetting his supposed faults and failures, and being humbly thankful that in his musings he finds some joy in being aware of just being alive.

Enjoy his reflections. May you someday have the pleasure of meeting the man himself. Jim has found some peace on his path of life. May you find peace on your path, too.

>Robert Ahrens
>Evanston, Illinois
>January, 2002

From **The Pits to the Pits**
By James A. Goulding

Part I

"The First Pit"

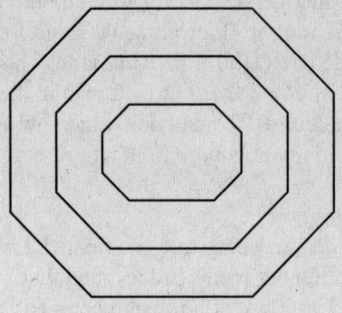

"Dying is easy, it's living
that scares me to death"
-Annie Lennox

Chapter 1

-And all you touch and all you see
is all your life will ever be.
   Pink Floyd

"Come back tomorrow and you can start"

On September 7th 1979, I walked onto the chaos of the trading floor in the Chicago Board of Trade (CBOT) for the first time. The day before I was hired on the spot by a man in the first office I walked into. "Come back tomorrow and you can start", said my new boss. Suddenly I was a REFCO runner.

I never intended on going into the financial industry, far from it. It almost seems predestined that I ended up at CBOT and applied for a job at a company called REFCO. Had I not walked into their offices I never would have risen as fast as I did, nor become as successful. An unlikely chain of events brought me to their door.

In August 1979, I had been accepted at the California Culinary Academy, a chef school in San Francisco. The school was only two years old but had a great reputation, and I was eager to start. Unfortunately, I had just missed their semester deadline. The next date I could begin was in April 1980. Nine months later.

So I had nine months to wait before starting my culinary career. What to do? Party, that's what. That's exactly what I intended on doing – and maybe work part time to earn party money.

Another thing happened to change the course. When I was in San Francisco applying at the Culinary Academy, I stayed with my sister and her husband. One night I borrowed my sister's car. I filled up the tank and proceeded to rip off the passenger-side front fender on a stationary pole as I was pulling out of a gas station.

After I returned the car and explained what happened, my sister and her husband thought for quite along time about what to do. They talked to my parents about what to do. The final answer came down in late August. Jim has to pay $475 for the damage. That amount may as well have been a million dollars. Minimum wage back then was about $2.75 and hour. Our economy was in pretty bad shape, too. Remember? Inflation was about 14% and no one was hiring. So my parents paid my sister and her husband, and then told me that I had to get a job while I was waiting to attend school. I could pay them back at $25 per week. Yikes! It was time to find a full-time job.

My job experience at that time had come from three places. My first job was at a McDonalds when I was fourteen, then another McDonalds and finally a family restaurant.

That night I went out to drown my sorrows in beer with friends. I related the story about my current debt position and how I didn't want to flip burgers for nine months, to my friends. One of them spoke up and talked about a great job she had as a 'runner' at the Chicago Mercantile Exchange (CME), working for a company named REFCO. That name stuck with me, along with the exciting visuals she put into my head of the trading floor. This was my first introduction to the world of trading and commodities.

I struggle with fate. Is there a pre-written destiny for us? I don't know. But in retrospect it amazes me how many things had to fall into place to set me onto a course leading to the CBOT. What are the probabilities that all of these events could have occurred, one after another? I'm not going to think about it. My head would explode.

For instance, when I went to find a job at the CME, I mysteriously ran into a neighbor of mine. When I got off the 'El' train I had no idea where I was. I could have been two blocks form the Sears Tower for all I know. Actually, I *was* two blocks form the Sears Tower. Anyway, I went down the stairs to the street level to get my bearings. That's when I spotted my neighbor. I told him I was going to look for a "runner" job, and I asked him where the CME was. He told me how to find it, but then he told me that the CBOT was closer. He pointed at a huge, concrete, Art-Deco building just two blocks away and said, "You might as well go to the CBOT first." I wanted to know what the difference was between the CME and the CBOT. "Nothing", he said.

Actually, for me at any rate, there were many differences between the CME and the CBOT. I never would have been a success in the trading industry so quickly, or at all for that matter, if I'd gone to the CME instead of the CBOT. Years later, I was to learn just how differently the CME operated.

Without going into much detail, I'll just state that the Corporations run both the CME and the trading floor of the CME, but the CBOT is much more independent.

The lower rung corporate jobs on the trading floor were fine: runners jobs, phone clerk jobs, out-trade checking jobs, etc., but once you advance through the ranks and it is your time to become a member of the exchange, you need to start kissing corporate CME butt. I now know I would have never lasted inside CME at that young age. I just didn't have what it took to jump though their corporate hoops. That just wasn't me. They would have fired my ass. I had a tendency to challenge the status quo.

Although the industry was starting to take off, and was in the process of expanding its employment base, not everyone was hiring. In fact, most had completed their hiring in August in anticipation of the college crowd going back to school. I would have probably struck out at the CBOT that day trying to locate a runner's job at other companies. I do not think I would have gone back downtown looking for another job at the exchanges. I wasn't thrilled with the idea in the first place. I wasn't a downtown type of guy. But there was one more twist of fate waiting for me – walking into the offices of Refco.

Refco stands for **R**ay **E**. **F**riedman **Co**mpany, is still very successful, but not widely known outside the commodity industry. Refco is a company that has many entrepreneurial thinkers. That's exactly what I am, entrepreneurial. I would have flopped at almost any other company. I fit into Refco just fine Plus, my first boss at Refco, Jay, would later stop me from quitting the industry three months into my runner's job.

I owe much of my success to Jay who was my first boss. Jay was very patient with me and continually supported me while I learned the business. Further credit to Tom Dittmer, who is related to Ray Friedman. Tom would take the company to the heights it currently enjoys.

Had all of these things not come together--it would have been back to sizzling burgers.

Chapter 2

-You gotta be crazy, you gotta have a real need.
   Pink Floyd

"The Floor"

I showed up on time my first day at work. It was easy, considering that I lived only 10 miles away in Oak Park. It was a very short El ride downtown. When I arrived at the CBOT, I punched in at Refco's CBOT office in the basement. Then I went out the door and hit the up button on the elevator to go to the 4th floor, where all the CBOT trading took place. When I set foot on the trading floor for the first time, I was astounded. The trading floor was mind blowing chaos of noise and sight. I'd never experienced anything like it.

From the moment I set foot on the floor, I knew I had found my domain. I was looking at a 19,000 sq. ft. space. Craning my neck I could see the ceiling four stories above me. The noise was exhilarating. People were everywhere and they were moving from one place to another in seeming pandemonium. This was the 'grain floor,' where soybeans, corn, soy meal, wheat, oats, silver, soy oil and a few other commodities were traded.

There were two huge electronic price boards on the grain floor, on the east and west walls. The background of the electronic boards was black with the prices reading out in bright orange. You could see any commodity trading on any exchange in the world on either of the two gigantic boards. The CBOT installed the electronic wallboards in 1967, enabling price-reporting time to be cut to seconds, and replacing chalkboard markers and Morse code clicks.

Underneath the boards, about 15 feet off the ground, was a catwalk where the old chalkboards were still in place. These chalkboards were the way they used to report recent trades. Not any longer! We had moved to the beginning of the computer age and the commodity industry was reaping the rewards of faster and faster information. The CBOT was just beginning to see those rewards manifest.

Here I was on the world's largest commodity trading floor at age of 17. Little did I know what lay ahead - riches beyond my wildest dreams, trading success and the admiration of my family, friends and peers. Waiting for me were exotic vacations, fast cars, fine restaurants and limos, limos, limos.

The CBOT was an environment that fit all of my abilities perfectly. To succeed on the floor you had to have certain behavioral qualities. It didn't matter if you had a MA, MBA, PHD or any other degree. If you had the ability to multi-task, problem solve and organize, you were on your way. Sure there was more to it, but those basic skills were the building blocks.

At the age of 17 I had no idea that I'd been born with these skills, but I was about to find out. I was also about to discover my weaknesses – like a lack of self-control. The lack of that one skill would destroy my health, lead me to attempt suicide and ruin my career. The saying goes, "If I only knew then what I know now"!

* * *

After receiving some guidance from other people walking to and fro on the floor, I found Refco's trading desk amidst the chaos. The organization of a commodity company's trading floor operations flowed like this, from lowest duties to highest: runner, phone clerk/out-trade checker, assistant floor Manager, floor manager.

Trading companies run their operations from desks that are aligned in rows that jut out vertically from the walls, and continue inward toward the octagonal-shaped trading pits.

The desks are lined with phones, which are always ringing. In the 17-years I spent on the trading floors of the CBOT, those phones never stopped ringing. Most of the phones where manned by phone clerks. Office traders (people trading off the floor) would phone in an order to buy or sell a certain quantity of, and a certain trading month of, a commodity, and the price at which they wanted the order to be executed. A phone clerk would answer the phone and write down the order on a small order ticket. If someone wanted to buy 5,000 bushels of soybeans, the order ticket would read: Buy 5 Nov SB 568. In other words: buy me 5,000 bushels of November soybeans at $5.68 a bushel.

There would also be a specific order number and a customer's account number on the ticket. After the phone clerk took the order, he/she would time stamp it, using a time stamping machine that sat at the desks by the phones. After this the ticket would go to a runner – like me.

The time stamp machines make a very annoying clicking noise at the top of every minute. There are hundreds of them on the trading floor. The phones would never stop ringing, the stamp machines never stopped clicking, and it all added to the bewildering cacophony.

The order ticket was always time stamped on the front when it left the desk and on the back when it returned. There are several reasons for this, the most important being a time reference for every single order's starting point and finishing point on the floor. Then, if there is a problem during a transaction, the assistant floor manager or the floor manager can go and listen to tapes of the conversation in an attempt to figure out what went wrong. Every single phone on the floor is tape-recorded. This is a necessary security precaution should disputes arise.

For example, if someone was entering an order they could say "buy" when they really meant "sell". Maybe somebody contends that they said buy at $5.68, but the phone clerk heard buy at $5.68 1/2, or vice versa. It happens all the time. With stakes high, speed a priority, and with the chaos of the floor, it's not surprising.

If a problem occurs at a company's trading desk on the floor it is called an "error". If a problem occurs in the trading pit between two traders it is called an "out-trade". Both problems can have destructive consequences. Out-trades can cost a trader their seat and their bank account. Phone clerks can lose their jobs due to an error. Errors and out-trades are four-letter words on the floor.

My job was to run between the incoming orders at the Refco desks to the Trading Pits. Now that you have a basic idea of how an order gets executed, let's return to my first day just before the opening bell.

Chapter 3

-So, so you think you can tell Heaven from Hell?
   Pink Floyd

"And They're Off!"

The clock read **9:29:00** in big red digital letters. There were four such clocks on the floor. Two on the north wall and two on the south. Another Refco runner, who was standing by me, tapped me on the shoulder and told me to get ready. The last cigarettes where doused out. (You could smoke on the floor in those days, but only before the market opened and after it closed). The 2,000 or so people on the floor got very quiet. By **9:29:55**, it was a dead hush except for the ticking of the time stamp clocks and the ringing phones. At exactly **9:30:00,** the place erupted.

A school-type bell went off and every trader in the room started screaming. I jumped about four feet in the air and looked around scared waiting for someone to attack! In the trading pits arms where waving and legs where thrusting the bodies of grown men straight up into the air as they tried to get the attention of other traders in the pit. It was pandemonium.

Every day starts like this in the world of "Open Out-Cry" commodity trading. I think at that exact point in time I knew I'd never be going to San Francisco to become a chef. This was where I wanted to be. These people were completely out of their minds, and so was I. I turned to the runner who had tapped me on the shoulder and smiled. He simply replied, "Cool, huh"?

***

"COME ON!" Came the shout from three feet away. A phone clerk was handing an order to my trainer. He grabbed the order and shot out from between the desks very quickly, blurting out "Let's go!" to me as he ran away.

I was only supposed to follow my trainer, look and learn. I trailed behind him as he ran towards the corn pit. There were people everywhere, running every which way.

Every person who came on the floor wears a jacket. It is more like a smock, but they are called trading jackets. That is, if you're a trader, it's called a 'trading jacket'. If you're a runner, it's called a smock.

Most runners wear gold colored jackets. This is the trademark of the runner, but some of the jackets range from conservative to bizarre.

The bizarre and brightly colored jackets are reserved more for the traders. The idea is to attract attention. If a trader stands out in the trading pit, they are apt to get more trades, which means make more money. Not too many of the companies go overboard with colors though. Refco's was brown. UPS brown. Today I was in runner gold.

As we got closer to the corn pit, the noise from it started to increase. I had this low level rush of adrenaline moving through my body, which started to increase as we moved closer to the pit. We arrived quickly, and my trainer took a very sharp right and disappeared into a sea of waving arms, screaming men and all out mass chaos. I did my best to stay with him. Steps, leading up and into the trading pit, appeared out of nowhere. I followed the gold jacket in front of me, up the steps and quickly realized what I had just stepped in the middle of....

"SELL IT AT THE ORDERS!"
"SOLD SOLD SOLD!!!!!!"
"HALF BID FOR 100, HALF BID!"

The pit was buzzing! Humming with excitement. Men where jumping up and down and screaming at the top of there lungs. I was stunned, excited, exhilarated, lost, confused and knew that I belonged right in the middle of all this.

The corn pit was octagon-shaped as most trading pits are. It had four steps tiered up on the outside of the pit and about eight doublewide steps going down into the center of the pit. So the center of the pit was actually lower than the whole trading floor itself. At this moment in time, you could not see the steps of the corn pit. They were covered with men. Every inch of space was taken up, except for some very narrow aisles inside the pit for runners, such as myself.

It was hot inside the pit. It was thick with clear-cut fear! You could smell it, and the excitement - that absolute basic savagery that every man is born with. This was primal. It was alive and thriving right here in the corn pit of the Chicago Board of Trade! The volume of the voices' crescendos higher then ebbed down to a level not of silence but of clear anticipation. What were they all waiting for in those few seconds of low volume?

Then, hundreds of voices exploded all at once! These men where jumping, twisting, turning and throwing their arms into the air yelling…

"SOLD!" "SOLD!"
"SELL a 1000 at 52 even!"
Their trading jackets flying about their bodies, unconcerned about the things that where flying out of the pockets onto the floor. It was madness.

My trainer was yelling and waving me over to him. He was standing just a few feet away, yet I could barely hear him over the din. I quickly hopped to his side and tried my best to listen to his explanation.

"This is our Dec-Corn-Broker. Just give the order to him when it's for December Corn. He'll let you know if you should stick around and wait for him to fill it. You'll get to know the types of orders you should hang around for. Don't worry about that now."

We headed out of the corn pit, running back to Refco's trading desk. I was jumping out of my skin. What was this? What where all those guys yelling about in there? What will it take for me to do that? These thoughts dashed through my head one after the other. Over and over I thought 'this is great!'

Back at the desk the phone clerks were on the phones busy taking orders and handing them to the runners. The rest of my first day would concentrate on learning what commodity was being traded in which pit and how those pits where broken down into trading months. Then, I would have to learn *exactly* who was to receive a particular order. Here I was multi-tasking, handling multiple projects and problem solving on my first day. I was so lucky and had absolutely no idea.

My first day ended abruptly at 1:15pm. That's the time the closing bell rings in the grain room. The pace quickly died down to a jog from a constant one-minute mile. It was like everyone started a cool down after a long workout. The cigarette smoke rose from every corner of the trading floor at exactly **1:15:01**. There were a few activities to complete after the bell, but as quickly as that bell rang the adrenaline rushed out of my body.

Chapter 4

-I can't wait to share this new wonder,
the People will all see its light.
   Rush

"My First Day Ends"

I headed off the floor and down to the Refco's office located in the basement or A-level of the CBOT. Of course, I wasn't the only one leaving the floor. It was a mass exodus. Not everyone at once, but in huge waves, hundreds and hundreds at a time. The elevator hallways on the 4th floor filled quickly. I would soon learn that the Refco employees went to the bank of elevators that were labeled 1-14. These were the only ones that headed to A-Level or the first basement level in the CBOT.

The elevator door opened, and I stepped off with some of my co-workers. I headed into Refco's office and slid my punch card into the machine. With a time stamp, I was done for the day. I had experienced so much. I had met so many wonderful people, and I was on a high.

Back on the ground floor of the CBOT, the revolving doors spun me out onto Jackson Street. The fall was arriving, and the afternoon temperatures were on the decline. The downtown lunch crowd was finishing up and heading back into their offices for the afternoon's work. Not me, I was done. The life of a grain room runner! Start late, leave early!

The El ran me home in its unstable, rickety way. I got home earlier than my parents. They wouldn't arrive until 5:30. I am the youngest of six. My one brother and three of my sisters were grown and gone. My 18-year-old sister was at college. I was the only one in the house.

I couldn't contain my excitement, so I got high.

My room was on the third floor of an 80-year-old house in Oak Park, IL. The whole 3rd floor was mine. I had a kick-ass stereo system and a great paraphernalia kit. I put my Rush album on and dug out my kit. My Rush album sleeve was perfect for deseeding marijuana. After I rolled a joint, cranked open the window, leaned out onto the street and fired up!

As I deeply inhaled I thought about what I'd just experienced the last 7 hours. I was so pumped! I'd found *it*. I'd found where *I belonged*! After four years of hell called High School, I was finally coming into my own. In Dante's masterpiece he missed one level of hell. It was Oak Park River Forest High School (OPRF). I think it was next to the river Styx. Or maybe it was in the ninth circle? Yes, it had to be the ninth, where Satan himself lived.

You must understand what it is like for me to enter the halls of OPRF. My teenage acne breakout started a bit earlier than most, seventh grade for me, so I was primed with craters and whiteheads by the time I entered my freshman year at OPRF. The older brother of one of my best friends said I'd have to run into brick walls if I had any chance of popping my zits. AAARGH! I was plagued. My body was one big zit. It grew like a weed from my face onto by neck, chest and back. It was a constant killer of my self-confidence.

High School is tough enough, as we all know. Give severe acne to someone like me, who fights the structure of the school system, and we have a disaster waiting to happen. It happened.

At OPRF you must get 8 credits a year to graduate or 32 credits over four years. I got 8 my first year. Then the bottom fell out. 2 credits sophomore year and 3 credits my junior year. I was only a full year behind by the time I reached my senior year! I received so many "F's" in my 2nd and 3rd year, I thought…nothing. It never crossed my mind that it was a problem - until my mother told me, just as I was about to enter my senior year, that I'd have to go to a FIFTH year of H.S. I almost choked to death right there. Ack! This was the ultimate wake up call and where I'd learn about one of my greatest assets. That asset is "When my back is up against a wall, I kick ass!"

I entered my senior year brainstorming. How was I going to do two-years worth of work in a single year, when I couldn't even complete a years worth of work in a year? It all fell into my lap one day. The whole thing. Like it was meant to happen. It began in, of all places, investments class.

We had picked a stock to buy in the class and sold Fuller Brushes to raise the money to buy the stock. That particular day we had finished our assignment early, and our teacher let us leave the class early. I was heading down the hallway that led to an outside smoking area for the kids. My Dean comes out of nowhere, walking around a corner.

He asked me, "Where are *you* going?" He knew my history of great studying and of applying myself.

I replied that I was "Going for a smoke."

"But...aren't you supposed to be in Investments class?", (How did he know that?)
"Mr. Buchanan let us go early," I defended myself.

I then received *the look*. Then *the hand* grabbed my arm. Then I'm being dragged into his office. The Dean said he'd call the teacher and ask him if what I said was true. I protested the whole way. I told him that if he called the teacher, he'd just deny it. When we got to my dean's office, he called the teacher, who immediately denied that he'd let the class out early. Surprise. I was pissed. I'd had it with the whole system. I told my Dean I was going to "XP".

XP was an acronym, for 'Experimental Program'. The program encompassed a few rooms, stuck in the northwest corner of the High School and was basically a program run by ex-hippies. I don't care what anyone else says, they were ex-hippies. Not to say that's bad, they were actually the smartest people in the whole system. You see, XP was right-brained. I had no idea back then, but that's what XP was about, teaching to the creative and intuitive side of a person, and the teachers in XP knew exactly what they where doing. They taught with pictures and a completely different structure than the norm.

It worked. I excelled, and I completed two-years worth of work in my final year of H.S. I worked hard and received all 16 credits that year for a 4-year total of 32. That's what I needed to graduate. This was my first glimpse that I wasn't a moron, as the school system seemed to want me to believe.

During those years my parents could only cross their fingers. They could only pray that I'd get through chef school, somehow, and make something of myself. To be fair, I wasn't the greatest teenager. I rebelled a tad more than Jim Morrison, so what were they left to think? As my five older siblings went to and completed college, I was obviously doomed when it came to academics. They were tired of raising kids, and I certainly wasn't making it any easier on them. I didn't intend them any harm, I was the center of the universe, and constantly had to remind them of that.

* * *

When my parents arrived home that night I sauntered down the stairs from my oasis on top of the house, trying to act cool. It wasn't long before my excitement bubbled over, and I related what my first day was like on the Floor of the Chicago Board of Trade. My parents stared at me with the corners of there mouths slightly turned up as if to say, "We are really happy for you Jim, but we wonder just how you're going to mess it up." They glanced back and forth at each other, and despite their half-smiles, were probably thinking something like, "We may yet escape having to pay for the this one's college tuition! YES!" Regardless of whatever they were thinking or whatever they said after I left that conversation, I left with the feeling that they were excited for me. That seemed important to me at the time.

Chapter 5

*-...and hop the Turbine Freight,
To far outside the Wire.*
        Rush

"We're going where?"

I spent the next few months learning the ropes as a runner, getting used to the rhythms of the floor and my co-workers. I made mistakes and took them very personally. It was like a stab in the heart every time I messed up. At that time I didn't know enough to realize that making mistakes is a normal part of the learning processes, and my self esteem was already at risk.

Nevertheless, my boss, Jay, liked what he was seeing, and so he offered me an opportunity to take on extra responsibility. He asked if I wanted to work after the market closed running documents between the exchanges and Refco's different offices in the loop. That vote of confidence made an impression on me, and I was happy to get a bigger check. This is exactly when I learned about the world of overtime. Refco paid time and a half. Do the same work and get paid 50% more. It seemed like a complete no-brainer to me.

The first hook was how good it feels to gain someone's respect. The second hook was the prospect of more money. The trap was putting more pressure on an immature psyche.

But I digress. We'll get back to this stuff later. Instead, let me tell you about the next big hook.

* * *

It was about the middle of November 1979, two months into my runner's job, that I first heard about *IT*!

IT was VEGAS.

One day, after I'd finished up with my new afternoon responsibilities, I was on my way to the El for my journey home, when someone called out my name.

"Hey Jim!", he started "Are you getting excited about Vegas?"

I whipped around and saw that it was Frank, a fellow runner.

Frank was a wonderful guy. I couldn't tell if he was a teenager or an adult at that time, because all Italians past the age of 12 looked like men to me. He started "running" with me about a week after I started at Refco. Frank and I would climb the ranks together and forge a wonderful friendship. Tragically he was killed in an auto accident in the Bahamas, while on vacation in the early 80's.

Frank and I both rode the El on the way home, so as we climbed the steps up to the platform I asked him what he was talking about. His face lit up. He opened his arms and put on his best Italian accent.

"Vegas, Jim. Capisce?"

"I do not Capisce, Frank", I replied in a very bad accent. "What are you talking about?"

We paid our fare and waited for the train. The November winds were picking up and it was already starting to get dark.

Frank continued, "Every year Refco takes it's employees out to Vegas for a weekend, as a kind of thank you."

He was smiling so wide I thought he was going to burst. He knew I'd be excited to hear this and was eagerly anticipating my reaction.

"Get the fuck outta here," I said and mock-pushed him back against the railing, the one guarding us from a neck-breaking fall onto Van Buren St.

"No shit, no lie," he said.

"When?", I asked, about to jump a 100 feet in the air.

"First week in December!" he declared as he shot me the high five and I obliged.

The El was coming around the bend towards the platform. I cranked up my voice to shout over the racket of the El.

"What's the deal" I yelled. "How do we get there? Where do we stay? WHO PAYS?", I continued as we boarded The train.

We found a seat and began our journey home. Frank lived up north so he'd be getting off the El in about 5 stops to transfer to a different train.

"You aren't gonna believe this. First they send a couple of busses to pick us up outside the CME building. Of course, they stock them with tasty alcoholic beverages. We all pile into the buses, and they take us to O'Hare where we get onto a charted 747." (There were four stops left).

I looked at him in amazement.

"Does chartered mean it's all ours?" I asked.

"ALL OURS!" he yelled and paid no attention to the others glancing towards us, envying our happiness after their particular day in "Office Hell".

"Then what"? (Three stops left).

"Disembark in Las Vegas airport." Frank said. "Buses pick us up there and take us to the Union Plaza hotel. It's in downtown Vegas. I hear that Ray Friedman owns a stake in it."

"So we stay in the Union Plaza? And what do we have to pay for all of this?" I asked waiting for the boom to drop.

Frank held up his hand, indicating "zero" and said, "Zippo!" (Two stops left).

"I can't believe this Frank. Why in Gods name would they do this? I can't imagine what it costs to rent a 747 let alone everything else."

"Jim, do you have any idea what kind of money Refco makes?" He said, looking at me. (One stop left).

I shook my head from side to side.

"Huge. Big, big, big. Tom Dittmer is one of the richest people in the U.S., and Tom has always shared his wealth with his employees."

"How big is big, Frank?" I asked dumbfounded.

"He's worth at least a couple of hundred MILLION."

He mouthed the last word like we'd say "billion" today. He got up and walked towards the door. His stop was coming up.

"This is unbelievable." I said to him in awe.

The doors opened and he stepped off waving goodbye, leaving me to ponder this VEGAS thing.

I'll remember that El ride for as long as I live. Never mind that the reality of riding the El trains in Chi-town or N.Y. They were a death trap and a hoodlums' home away from home. People even occasionally find themselves out on the tracks suddenly facing a speeding train, perhaps wondering:

"Why did that Fucker push me…" Splat.

"How did I get out…Oh, shi…" Splat.

No, I knew nothing of this. Any of it. I was an oblivious 17-year-old, cruising along to the rhythmic clickety-clack with a big ol' VEGAS grin on my face. As I stared out at the darkening sky as we crossed the Chicago River, this incredible excitement welled up inside of me. A million visions flooded my brain. I could barely contain myself.

Chapter 6

-To seek the sacred river Alph
To walk the caves of ice
To break my fast on honeydew
And drink the milk of Paradise.
     Rush

"Vegas"

We hopped on the buses and grabbed a seat. It was Friday, December 7, 1979, and we were embarking on a weekend jaunt to Sin City. Oh yes, one other thing. I had a pocket full of money. Refco was kind enough to give us our Christmas bonus before we left. How cool was that?

The day before we left, Jay called me into his office and handed me an envelope saying, "This is just a little gift from Tom." I opened it, and there was a check for $400. I was stunned. I looked at Jay and said, "And he takes us to Vegas, too?" Jay looked toward the front door of his cubbyhole office and yelled, "So someone actually appreciates this?" I turned expecting to see someone standing there, but there was no one. I didn't get that he was making a point about some people taking it for granted.

"Good for you, Jim," Jay said, getting up from his desk and stepping out in front of it to pat me on the back. I felt tears well up in my eyes. I know, I know. Silly. But it meant a lot to me to have Jay's approval. I would seek that elusive approval thing from many father-type figures down at the CBOT over the next 17 years. Jay was the first.

So I had 400 smokers burning a hole in my pocket and my friends were passing a cooler my way filled with quality beer – Heineken, Michelob, St. Pauly's - heaven. I was in heaven.

I had forged some wonderful friendships since I began three months ago. I had earned respect from my peers and bosses for being a hard worker, someone who showed up every day and on time.

I also started to learn that it was OK to party heavily, but only after work, and "You better show up the next day, or you're gone!"

* * *

We arrived at the airport quickly for a Friday afternoon and fell off the bus into the terminal. There was someone waiting for us who actually knew where they were going - our guide to the plane. Having a leader was a good idea, because many of us were already buzzed. They must have done this before, I thought.

Our leader guided us to the gate and right onto *our* plane - *no one else's*! *Our very own 747*! I couldn't believe it.

The flight was great fun. A true party at 37,000 feet. We landed in Las Vegas about 4 hours after take-off.

While we walked from the plane through the ramp-way and into the concourse, it became very apparent we were not in Kansas anymore. It was warm. It was desert dry and smelled of fresh air. I couldn't get over this new sensation. I had never experienced a climate like this. Yes, I had traveled before, destination the northeast. It was in the back of a 1969 Ford station wagon with five brothers and sisters. But, this dessert air was a brand new experience for me. It was like I was a modern day explorer experiencing something wonderful and different.

As we walked through the concourse, I was taken aback by a sound coming from all around us. I sought out the source, and to my delight, it was coming from banks of slot machines. They were everywhere, and the people playing them were excited! The anticipation on their faces reminded me of the traders in the pits.

We boarded the buses and headed to the hotel. The Union Plaza jumped out at us as we turned into downtown Vegas. It stood three blocks down. Immediately, it reminded me of the Chicago Board of Trade that anchored the 'Financial Canyon' in Chicago.

The bus finally came to a halt in the front of our temporary home for the next two days, and we spilled out into the lobby. Room numbers and roommate assignments were handed out very orderly. We dispersed quickly to discover our new digs. But before we headed up, we were told to be in the ballroom in one hour, dressed to the nines for a cocktail party. Cocktail party? That's exactly what we all needed: more drinks. I quickly got dressed in the only suit I owned and went to the cocktail party downstairs.

My boss Jay pulled many of the runners aside just before the party got started and told us to act like gentlemen, or he'd kill us when we got back. Every runner had a great deal of respect for Jay, so they took it to heart and behaved accordingly. Everyone was on their best behavior. Looking fabulous and being extremely courteous to each other. This was not the trading floor.

The cocktail party ended without incident, and the real fun was about to begin, gambling!

As I stepped into the casino it was like the first day I saw the grain floor in Chicago. It was electrifying! Bigger and better than my wildest dreams. The roulette table, black jack, craps, blinking lights and people moving about in a chaotic ocean. Rows of one-arm bandits were strategically placed around the floor. There were men in suits, standing with arms crossed, looking stone-faced and worried, as if the President of the United States was about to arrive. Suddenly a roar from a three-deep group around a craps table. Madness all over again!

Off I went to try my luck. The moment I stepped up to the blackjack table, I was asked, by a very scantly clad woman, if I'd like a drink. This was too good to be true. "Yes please, Heineken." I was living large.

* * *

The sun shone between the curtains. Bright desert sun. My head was pounding. My stomach was vowing to give back what little I put in it the day before. This was the hangover from hell.

Most times I escaped these brutal backlashes as many other 18-year-olds do. But I broke the cardinal rule. I had not eaten much the day before; furthermore, I was a smoker. Combining nicotine and alcohol with an empty stomach is the kiss of death. This would prove to be my demise for the next 8 hours. At some miserable point I went back to sleep.

I awoke later to see Eric, my assigned roommate, asleep in the other bed. I don't know how long he'd been there. He was out like a light. I rolled over and tried to go back to sleep, only succeeding after I got up and downed two aspirin.

The sun was still shining through the drapes when I re-awoke, but the shadows in the room had moved. I glanced at the clock and at the other bed. It was 2:00 pm, and Eric was gone. Thankfully, I was feeling much better. As I started to climb out of bed the door suddenly opened and Eric strolled in looking very happy.

"You're alive!" He shouted, laughing at me and plopping on his bed. "Lets go."

"Alright, alright," I said, working my way toward the shower.

"Where are we going?" I yelled from the bathroom.

"The Strip!" He shouted back.

When I came out of the shower Eric pulled a little surprise from the pocket of his jeans. It was a vile packed with coke. After snorting some lines, he handed me the vile saying, "Keep it. I've got plenty." I shoved it in my pocket and gave him a high-five!

We hopped in a cab in front of the Union Plaza. We were headed to the strip. Downtown Vegas was quite the spectacle but didn't even come close to the lights and ambiance of the Strip, which was electric from the lights to the people. Huge neon signs dwarfed the hotels and announced popular comedians and musicians playing at that locale. It was magic.

Eric told the driver to drop us at Caesar's Palace. As we got closer, Eric pointed it out. The building was beautiful, very blue, big and mysterious. Not a window could be seen. We exited the cab and headed in. The casino doors opened to a grand entryway with four or five steps leading up into the lobby. It was the biggest casino on earth, with a gaming floor that spread out in all directions.

"Let's hit the craps table," Eric said.
He started walking toward a table. I followed with a bit of protest.

"Eric, I don't know how to play craps."

"I'll teach you," he said. "Just do what I do."

Craps. What a confusing game, especially when you're drinking and snorting coke. I just followed Eric's lead. He moved his chips fast and furious. I followed, and my chips starting stacking up, $300, $400, $500. My heart was pounding with each roll of the dice and each trip to the bathroom to snort more coke.

Cocaine brought a whole new mania to drinking. The more I snorted the more I could drink, and the higher I got. What could be better than this? Vegas, beautiful, scantly-clad women, coke, booze? Eric was happy; I was happy; the other people at the craps table were happy. I felt like I'd never felt before. Vegas had its hooks in me. So we gambled and partied until 7:30 am.

* * *

The buses were leaving at 10:00 am. We had two hours to get packed and get our butts out in front of the Union Plaza. No problem, since we had few belongings with us. We even had time to have some breakfast.

What a different plane ride on the way home - very subdued. A few people played cards. A couple even had some beer, but most slept. People were strewn about haphazardly - legs dangling over armrests, bodies this way and that, the heads and necks of the passed out at unlikely angles, bouncing against window glass in occasional turbulence. Gee, do you think that everyone else had been doing the same thing Eric and I had been doing?

We landed at O'Hare, grabbed our luggage and boarded a bus. The bus deposited us in a very quiet and eerie downtown Chicago. Thankfully, Eric drove his car on Friday and it was close by. He lived in Oak Park, too, so he dropped me off at home, and I walked into my house late that Sunday like I was a king.

Chapter 7

-Come in here dear boy, have a cigar,
 you're gonna go far, fly high,
 you're never gonna die,
 you're gonna make it if you try;
 they're gonna love you.
          Pink Floyd

"Attention"

Something new was beginning to happen in my house. It was the first time that I could remember getting personalized attention, except when I was sick or in trouble. Now attention was being thrown at me like confetti because of this CBOT thing. Work and money was getting me attention.

I was the youngest of six children. By the time I became a teenager my parents were pretty tired of childrearing. Attention was not something easily come by in the house I grew up in. I was so needy for attention that even attention for getting into trouble was better than nothing.

You'll remember that my grades were a problem in high school. Well, that was the least of my problems. I had a few run-ins with the law, too. Some would call them more than run-ins.

When I was 15 years old I snuck out my second-story bedroom window at 2:00 am and shimmied down a tree. My grandmother's car was in our garage next to my Mom's. I haven't the foggiest notion why it was there that weekend, but I thought nothing of taking it out for a spin.

Off to my girlfriend's house I went. She snuck out the back door, and our plan was working just fine. We went to a 7-Eleven to get smokes and snacks, but on the way a police officer passed by on the opposite side of the road. He flashed his bright lights at me. I immediately searched for my bright lights switch to see if they were on, but I couldn't find the switch. Quickly, I glanced in the rearview mirror to see if the cop had made a u-turn. Thankfully, no. My girlfriend and I began the futile search for the damn switch but couldn't find it, so we finally gave up.

Guess who I ran into about 30 minutes later on the way back to drop off my girlfriend? That would be the very same officer we drove by earlier. He was headed directly toward me, and this time he made a little maneuver to let me know he wanted me to pull over. He not only flashed his bright lights again, but this time he slowly swerved toward me. There was plenty of room on the street to counter this maneuver. I didn't give it a second thought. After I cleared his car, I floored it. I saw the officer pull the deadly u-turn in the rearview, so I knew he was in pursuit.

We were off to the races through the darkened and, until then, quiet streets of Oak Park, Illinois. After five or six blocks of this, more police cars joined in the chase. Richard Petty, that was me. I handled the turns very well at speeds in excess of 50 mph, and I didn't even have a driver's license! I raced up one street, down another. I even raced through the alleys at over 100 mph!

It finally occurred to me that enough was enough. This was fun, but fun time was over. It was time to face the music. I pulled over and parked, about three miles from the start of the race. I had accumulated altogether eight Oak Park police cars.

Twelve-gauge shotguns appeared out of the patrol car windows. There were some very pissed officers at the other end of them. They were yelling at us! Can you imagine that? I don't remember what they where yelling, but it was something to the effect of, "Get your skinny asses out of the fucking car, NOW!"

We obliged. They turned the car upside down looking for drugs, guns, bodies –whatever, but this was my grandmother's car after all, and she hadn't smoked pot or killed anyone in years.

The most memorable part of it all had to be when a female officer approached my girlfriend and me, handcuffed in the back of a cruiser. She wanted to know what the deal was. Why did I run?

"I don't have a driver's license," I mumbled.

The look on the officer's face is still etched into my brain. A multitude of emotions were traveling through the forty-eight muscles of her face. It was a pained look. My best guess is, she was really pissed.

"Fuck!" She yelled, as she walked over to the other officers to share the revelation.

Attention is what I sought: attention is what I received. And I wanted more of it, so began my black sheep image. I built this image slowly and carefully. When it came to attention, I was not to be outdone by my sisters or my brother.

* * *

We stumbled out of the bar. It was two months after my final court appearance for behaving like Richard Petty on the streets of Oak Park. I received court supervision for a year. If I could stay out of trouble for the following year, my record would be clean. This meant absolutely nothing to me. I was out for attention, not pleasing some judge.

There were six of us that evening. A conversation ensued while we walked to the car.

"Let Jim drive," bellowed one of the males in the group.

"Yea, let Jim drive," seconded another.

It was my girlfriend's parents' big, honkin' 1975 Ford station wagon. Without a word, my girlfriend (same girlfriend) tossed me the keys. I gladly caught them and jumped into the driver's seat. By the time we were all situated, there were three in the front seat and three in the back seat.

I had no driver's license, I was 15-years-old, drunk and on probation. "Get your motor runnin'; head 'er on the highway".

The bar was just over the border in Chicago. The racecar driver that resided within me took off. We'd decided to head over to Eileen's house. The destination was about three miles away. It's amazing how many things can happen on such a short jaunt. Everything was going fine until the streets started to narrow a bit, with parked cars on both sides of the parkway. Toss in alcohol, and you can take a wild guess what happened next.

I sideswiped a brand-spanking-new, shiny red 1977 Camero. This would have been an easy get-away, but the Chevy belonged to a college student and he was standing bug-eyed about twenty-five feet away. He had just come out of a party and he wasn't alone. There must have been thirty other people exiting the party with him.

"Floor it!" Came a yell from the back seat of the Ford, and I did.

Two blocks later everyone in the car was screaming when I hit my second object for the night, a small tree in a yard. It was small enough that the Ford ran right over it. Since I had veered to the left side of the street, this meant I must veer back to the right side. I pulled the steering wheel hard and the car hurdled off the grass and back into the street…right into the back of a mint, classic 1966 Ford Mustang.

After rear-ending the Mustang I took out a lonely stop sign, just sitting there minding its own business. I gave the gas pedal a firm press, countered with a hard left on the steering wheel and ended up on a perfectly manicured lawn, tearing it to shreds. More gas, more pulling on the steering wheel, back down into the street, across the width of it onto another fresh lawn. Finally we cam to rest – in a house.

This was once a quiet little house on a quiet little street, nestled in a quiet little community. Because of me the house I smashed into became part of local folklore. It would be remembered for generations to come as *The*

House That Some Asshole Parked His Ford In. In five minutes, I'd managed to take out three cars, four lawns, a tree, a stop sign, and the front of a house, and I had created an urban legend. This would solidify my black sheep status and get me lots of attention.

While four of us rode in the back of the police paddy wagon (two got away), I told the sorrowful story of my probation that was handed down a few months earlier. In the most incredible display of friendship I have ever been on the receiving end of, one of my friends said he would take the blame.

"Are you kidding, John?" I asked this hero.

"No." was his simple reply.

And he lived up to that. His only requirement was my providing him with a lawyer. And I lived up to my end of the bargain.

Coincidentally, the lawns that were damaged were all under the care of the drummer in the small band I was playing in at the time. When he came to band practice four days after the fiasco, he told us, "Some crazy fuck tore up four of my lawns! What an asshole!"

"By the way, would you be willing to fix all the lawns for free?" I snuck in at the end of his story.

"No way," said my drummer.

"Yes way," I replied.

The '77 Camero, the house and the '66 Mustang were fixed and paid for by the insurance company that covered the Ford station wagon, right before they dropped my girlfriend and her family. It turns out that the Mustang was owned by a Chicago cop. My girlfriend's father just happened to be a Chicago cop. Furthermore, he knew the owner of the Mustang. No one showed up in court to file a complaint. The lawyer who I hired to defend my friend John did, and John received a slap on the wrist.

This would be my last run-in with the law, attention or not. I could clearly identify when I had horseshoe up my butt. Whether an angel was watching over me or if it was plain stupid luck, I'd learned my lesson.

Boy, did I receive allot of attention though!

* * *

I would turn this negative attention into what I thought was positive attention as I started climbing my way up the ladder at the CBOT. Later in life, after years of therapy, I'd come to realize that the kind of attention I got from making lots of money wasn't really what I was after either. At the time though, I couldn't believe my good fortune.

So far I was making my regular salary, plus overtime, and I got a generous check from Refco and a trip to Las Vegas. I was getting some positive feedback from my parents. It felt good.

Then, as we drew closer to Christmas Day, I began to pocket five, ten and twenty dollar bills from the brokers who I carried orders to throughout the trading floor. I took one of my co-workers aside and asked him why the brokers were giving me money. He said it happened every year. It was their way of saying thank you. This place was great, I thought. My total take in the three days before Christmas was an extra $400!

When I came home from work on Christmas Eve, my whole family had arrived to celebrate the holidays. They were all situated in the living room conversing. I stepped dramatically into the middle of the room and silently started pulling fives, tens and twenties from my pockets and let them float to the floor. I looked up at my siblings, one at a time, and saw the amazement on their faces.

"Do you believe this place I work at? Those bills are 'thank yous' from the brokers on the grain floor."

Their reaction taught me that I could get attention with money. I didn't have to be sick or get into trouble to receive it. I just had to make money. Right then and there I knew I'd be a success at the CBOT. There was never a doubt in my head from that day forward. Nothing would stop me from getting this hallowed attention.

This new goal of mine would put into motion the exact same cycle my father started when he was my age: sacrifice your health to achieve success in the business world. Never step on anyone or be unfair to anyone in business, but feel free to beat the crap out of yourself. That was perfectly acceptable.

Chapter 8

-Oh by the way, which one is Pink?
Pink Floyd

"Promotion and Out-trades"

On Friday, September 7, 1979, I started working at the CBOT. Exactly one year later on Monday, September 8, 1980, I was promoted to phone clerk. My running days were over, but not before I tried to quit.

In early 1980, I made a common runner's error. I forgot to pick up a very important sheet of paper after the market closed. It was my job to go get this piece of paper, which was about 5 blocks away from Refco's office, and bring it back. This piece of paper allowed the people in the office to complete their work and go home for the day. I brought back the wrong document and some of the guys in the office, including Jay, lit into me. They were pissed. I didn't take it well. I flew the five blocks back to get the piece of paper and returned with it. I was shaken by my dressing-down. I told Jay that I quit.

"Wait a minute." Jay said. "You do not want to do that. You're a good runner and have a lot of potential."

"I suck. I can't even pick up a piece of paper correctly." I said, very depressed and very disappointed in myself.

"Bullshit!" Jay said, standing up and moving towards me. He put his arm around me and walked me out of the office and into the hallway.

"Jim, you are gonna do fine. Don't worry about us giving you shit for fucking up. It's the nature of the business. People just give each other shit in this business."

"Well," I said, with my head pointed straight down at the floor. "I'll give it another try."

"Good, good," Jay said, slapping me on the back. "You'll do just fine!"

He walked back into the office after telling me to go home and come back the next day ready to kick some ass.

This was the final piece to the puzzle. The last of the very strange things that had to happen for me to start, stay and complete my career at the CBOT. I was ready to quit, but Jay stopped me. If he hadn't, I would not be writing this. I am, and always will be, indebted to Jay for that and many more things he did to guide me throughout my career.

* * *

The day I received the news of my promotion was a day of triumph and celebration. For the first time since I could remember, I would receive something wonderful from my father - *praise*.

My dad frequently dropped me off close to the CBOT in the morning and picked me up on lower Wacker drive in the late afternoon. When he picked me up that Friday afternoon, I shared the news with him.

He went wild! He couldn't believe it. He was so happy for me and so proud of me. He was practically jumping up and down!

"You didn't!" He said with a booming enthusiasm in his voice.

"I did," I said, soaking it up.

"Oh Jimmy! This is great! Congratulations!" He slapped me on the knee.

I will never forget that ride home. We were in Chicago rush-hour traffic, and it was as if we had the expressway to ourselves. There was nothing else happening outside the windows as far as I was concerned. I had the only thing that mattered to me…my father's attention and admiration.

The minute we got home, he jumped on the phone and started calling my siblings to report the news. I was stunned.

He told my mother the moment she came home from work. He was elated! I hadn't felt that close to him in the last ten years, maybe longer. It was a moment I will hold onto forever. It was a moment that I would try to duplicate over and over again, yet, somehow this eluded me. To me, the accomplishments I achieved over the following ten years seemed to pale in comparison. The more he denied *it* to me, the more I began to look in other places.

As a result of his adulation on this particular day, I went back to the CBOT to work even harder. I now had two motivations: to make money and get promoted. Both of those things would get me more praise from my father. At least that's what I thought then.

* * *

The following day, I began my training immediately. There was a catch. I was asked to leave the grain room trading floor and enter the bond trading room or 'The South Room'. The south room was small. If I remember correctly, it was 5,000 square feet as opposed to the grain floor which was 19,000 square feet. The south room opened in 1975 when the Government National Mortgage Association (GNMA) futures started trading. The thirty-year Treasury Bonds (T-bonds) were added to the south room on Monday, August 22, 1977, which would mark the most successfully launched futures contract ever.

My phone clerk trainer was Jerry, the floor manager in the south room. There were a couple of runners at Refco's desk in the south room also. My time spent working during the day, at Refco, would also increase. I'd get to work by 6:00 am to start trade checking and then I went to the T-bond floor to work the phones at 7:00 am until 2:00 pm. After that I'd have a 2-hour break until 4:00 pm then back to the office to do trade checking again, until 6:00 pm. This was my life for the next year and a half. So began my career in the bond market. So began the ever increasing pressure and responsibility that went with promotions. I was 18-years-old.

* * *

Out-trades are almost always losers, except for this one time in 1986. A guy I stood next to in the T-bond pit, who traded his own money (he would be called a *local* or *market maker*), had an out-trade that turned out to be a winner for him – a $133,000 winner to be exact. So he went out and bought a Ferrari Testarossa! I have a picture of it in my office, and it is a thing of beauty.

There was another unusual out-trade in the bond room that occurred in '84 or '85. This one was 'of the legend kind'. This guy walked up to a broker's assistant and gave him a verbal order to buy a large number of T-bonds. The order was big. The assistant got excited and didn't pay attention to the person who gave it to him. It turned out the person who gave the order to him was dressed in disguise. He was wearing a wig and a fake mustache. I kid you not. (To this day I do not know the details about the individual who committed this crime.)

In a case like this you need to look at the rules of the Chicago Board of Trade to determine whose shoulders a blunder like this falls on. The rule states that if you take a verbal order and no one claims that order the next day, you are liable for that order. The bottom line was, the broker had to take ownership of the T-bonds.

The following morning before the market opened, the broker was informed of this problem. No one had stepped up to claim the T-bonds he bought for the man in the disguise.

Brokers made their money by executing orders in the pit and then receiving a commission for each contract they bought or sold. Back in the 1984-85, the going rate was about $1.25 a contract. If a broker bought or sold one hundred contracts for a client, then he'd rack up $125.00 in commissions. This broker might have averaged 1500 to 2000 contracts a day. Sounds pretty good! However there's a caveat, errors and out-trades. One error or out-trade could cost you $100,000!

I'm not going to get into why. It's too complicated. Just know that the market was going to open at a point where the T-bonds this broker owned were going to cost him $100,000, very big money in the mid 1980's.

Lets add one more thing to the fire for this broker! The government was about to release a report that morning. The report would move the T-bond market. It would move it a lot. This particular report always did. It was the monthly release of the unemployment figures in the United States for the past month.

In 1984-85, we opened the T-bonds at 8:00 am, but the unemployment figures came out at 7:30 am. This would affect the opening price of the T-bonds in a very big way. This unfortunate broker was down 100k and knew it.

And so did everyone else on the floor. It doesn't take long for rumors to get floated around. We all knew that this broker was probably going to lose everything and be out of a job.

The Government released the report at 7:30 am. The implausible happened. The report made the T-bonds' opening price change direction and go in favor of the broker. The $100,000 loss was wiped out by the time we opened at 8:00 am and the broker recovered with a profit of $600,000!

He retired the next day. No joke.

* * *

After the market closed at 2:00 pm I had two hours free, until the Chicago Board of Trade Clearing Corporation (BOTCC) completed the matching of all the trades that took place that day on the exchange. What didn't match was kicked out of the computer and printed on a report. Each firm received one of those reports, containing all the out-trades that affected the traders who cleared that firm. (This was the piece of paper I forgot when I tried to quit and Jay stopped me.)

I'd head to 135 South LaSalle Street, where Refco's brand new headquarters were located. I would finish the day at about 6:00 pm. Lots of over-time. Putting in so many hours made for some big paychecks. I was making enough to move out of my parents' house.

In the summer of 1981, at the age of 19, I did just that. My internal drive was working overtime saying, "Achieve more, make more money, advance or you are worthless!"

Chapter 9

-Mama loves her baby,
 And Daddy loves you too
 And the sea may look warm
 And the sky may look blue.
   Pink Floyd

"On My Own"

I told some of my friends at Refco of my plans to fly the coop. One of them spoke up and asked if I'd like to sub-lease his apartment in Rogers Park. It was a neighborhood in northern Chicago. The apartment was small and on the third floor, but it would be my first place. As far as I was concerned, it was a palace.

I rented the apartment from a friend named Jeff. Now, there's a very interesting story about Jeff. After he left Refco, he ended up in the S&P futures trading pit at the Chicago Mercantile Exchange. He was in the S&P trading pit the day the market crashed on a Monday in October, 1987. Some readers may remember that day.

The Dow was at a low of 796 on August 20, 1982, but then started climbing quickly. It peaked at 2,746 on August 25, 1987. That was an astronomical increase by historical standards. Then, on October 19th, the Dow closed 508 points lower than the previous day, at 1738.

Jeff was in the S&P pit trading during on that fateful day. The S&P futures were rising and falling in huge swings. Massive amounts of money were being made and lost.

A broker bought one hundred S&P futures from Jeff as they were going down quickly. In about ten seconds, the S&P's had gone down so much Jeff made well over $1,000,000. In fact, he told someone that if he had dropped his pencil, he would have made two million. That's how fast the market dropped.

Now, this was conjecture until five years later when I went golfing with Jeff and asked if it happened. He said it did.

There were many fortunes made and lost that day. We'll come back to it in a later chapter because, for about three hours on "Black Monday", I thought I'd lost all of my money and more.

* * *

When I moved out of my house I was 19 years old. I fit everything I owned into a brown Toyota lift-back. I sublet the apartment from Jeff for about six months. It was a fantastic experience. I could do as I pleased. I also quickly learned what else moving out of my parents' house meant…more work – the laundry, the cleaning, the shopping and walking to the El in the morning.

I really didn't mind, though. As a matter of fact, when my sub-letting time was up I rented a huge apartment closer to Oak Park in the winter of 1981. I took meticulous care of my possessions and the apartment itself. This pissed off my Mother to no end. When I lived at home, I was a slob. The minute I move out, I became Felix Unger. She didn't believe it was my place when she first came over for a visit.
 "Who lives here?" She mused, staring at the spotless kitchen in utter disbelief.

I didn't know it at the time, but this new level of independence would help set me up for my eventual fall. For a 19-year-old kid I had an incredible amount of responsibility. On top of this I found myself in a social situation that I was simply not prepared for.

My new apartment was in Forest Park and close to the train. It was actually the basement floor of a house. The upper floor had been turned into an apartment and was also rented.

Right behind the house was a bar. The owner of the bar also owned the house. I quickly became friends with him. He was much older than me, but we were both Irishman and got along splendidly. I also got along quite well with his beverage offerings.

Moving up the ranks at Refco meant more responsibility. More responsibility meant more stress, and then there was the social atmosphere at the CBOT. For a young, socially inexperienced teen, it was brutal.

People cut each other down all the time, but they were only joking. It was a way to relieve stress and to air minor grievances without letting things get out of hand, but I didn't know how to play the game. I couldn't figure out why people treated each other with such disdain, nor could I figure out why they thought it was funny. When they made fun of me, it was like daggers embedding themselves into my soul. My self-esteem plummeted.

Self-hatred was very common to me by the age of 19. It was common in my Irish family. It was a way of life at the time. This self-hatred had a voice that countered whatever potential I had. It'd say, "Don't ever think you'll amount to a decent human being. You're ugly and stupid. Be grateful for the job and the few friends you have."

Without any constructive way of dealing with the job and social stress, I turned to what I knew. My drinking skyrocketed. Moving out of my parents' house and into my own apartment gave me the opportunity to hang myself. Soon, I'd add cocaine and other assorted drugs to the mix.

Chapter 10

-I can't explain, you would not understand
This is not how I am
I have become comfortably numb.
     Pink Floyd

"Cocaine"

Cocaine brought me the attention I craved, just as money had, and I could afford it. I was making excellent money because I was putting in so many hours, at least eleven hours a day, most days twelve - because the bond market was booming. I had instant friends, when I had coke with me.

Unfortunately the wonderful cocaine highs were coupled with dark bouts of depression.

* * *

The south room was exploding. Bonds were booming. The more volume the bonds did, the more people the room needed. Soon we'd be reaching peak capacity. At the same time my job confidence was growing.

The numbers being traded were staggering. No other commodity had ever seen this kind of volume. The bonds did 8.8 million contracts in 1980, and almost doubled to 16.3 million in 1981. In 1982, they did 19.8 million.

During this same period the grain room was declining in volume. It did 35.8, 32.1 and 27.2 million in 1980, 81 and 82 respectively. This affected morale, and so the crack was born inside the CBOT that would spider to a complete 'us against them' by 1984. It was literally the grains against the bonds.

Although the grains would recover from a dismal year of trading in 1982, they would never trade above 40 million contracts in the decade of the '80s and would average 30 million contracts a year throughout. The bond room would peak in 1989, with 79 million contracts traded, not including options contracts which were introduced in the bond room in 1982. If you add in options, the final score in 1989 was grains 35 million, bonds 101 million.

The bond people were making an enormous amount of money year to year, while the grain room's volume and salaries were declining.

* * *

I hear the screams from my bedroom – excruciating screams coming from the dining room. I gently laid the mirror onto the bed. I didn't want to spill any of the coke on it. I'd been drinking all day and snorting coke for two hours. I'd downed at least a case of beer by then and had no intention of stopping. When I walked into the dining room I felt – nothing. I glanced down to the dining room floor and saw Mike, holding his knee in a cradle position. He was rocking back and forth on his back and screaming in pain. When I finally got a closer look, I could see that everything below his knee was just dangling there, as if the bottom half of his leg were trying to come off. (Think Joe Theisman.) My friends were surrounding him, frozen with priceless expressions plastered on their faces, trying to figure out what to do. I calmly stepped over Mike, dialed 911 and requested an ambulance. After I hung up, I realized that a police car would accompany the ambulance.

I had a 2X3 foot mirror on my bed and it was full of blow - at least two- thousand-dollars worth. Forget that we were all under the drinking age. I could have cared less. But the blow was serious.

The thought of the police coming sent me into a very focused effort to get all of the cocaine out of plain sight. I collected all of the mirrors of coke in my apartment and put them on my bed. While I was doing this, my friends comforted Mike as best they could, but it was very ugly. He was in a great deal of pain. I just wanted to shoot him like a lame colt and end his misery.

I could hear sirens and they were getting closer. I took the whole-lot of cocaine and gently shoved it under my bed. There was no way I would spill a grain of this stuff, because I knew the second this whole mess was over and all the police, ambulance, fireman and whatnot left, I was going to party harder than ever. This was a perfect excuse, or so thought my determined coke and booze-marinated brain. As I rose from beneath the bed, the knocks on the door came.

The police showed themselves in without any help and went straight to the source of the agonized noises Mike was making. I greeted them as the owner and (while trying not to grind my teeth or let any other tics pop up that go along with cocaine use) began describing what had happened.

"Mike is a black belt in karate. He was showing my friend Brian a sidekick when Brian instinctively reached out and grabbed Mike's foot. Mike had had a few drinks and couldn't keep his balance. As he fell to the floor, Brian didn't let go of his foot. POP! Out came his knee. This all took place in about two seconds."

The policemen observed Mike lying on the dining room floor with tormented horror on his face.

"The ambulance should be here in minutes. What is this, a painting party?"

His inquiry made sense. I had been repainting the apartment that week. Ladders, paint cans, drop cloths and brushes where laid about. This was no painting party, of course, until the officer brought it up.

"Yes officer, that's exactly what it is." I answered. Others nodded in agreement.

I noticed that the other officer was checking out the other rooms in my apartment. It didn't bother me, until he walked into my bedroom. Trying to keep a calm demeanor while talking with one officer while the other walked into the bedroom was quite a feat. My heart was beating so hard I thought it was going to jump out and go for a run.

You can forget about asking for a warrant in this case. My mind couldn't go there. It's not like my internal lawyer kicked in and said, "Hey Jim, don't worry about what they find, because they don't have a warrant and anything they do find will be thrown out in court!" I was 20 years old and jacked up on coke and booze. The only thought running through my brain was, "You're fucked if they find that coke!"

The seconds ticked away like hours while that cop was in my bedroom. My friends covertly eyed each other, confirming that they were thinking the same thing I was, but our fear was all for naught.

The officer emerged from the bedroom with nothing in his hands and briskly walked by us to check out the kitchen. Why he didn't look under the bed, I'll never know. The only logical explanation was that my angel was with me.

The paramedics rushed in and followed the moaning to Mike. The cops backed off so the paramedics could work on Mike. The cops were feeling a great deal of sympathy for him - maybe the screaming helped, and besides, they were done with us.

One of the paramedics left to get the stretcher. The other tried to figure out just how they where going to get Mike from the floor and onto the stretcher without causing him more pain. In came the stretcher, and so began a half-hour process of moving Mike onto the gurney. The whole ordeal was cruel. The slightest movement of Mike's leg was sending horrifying pain through his body.

Finally, the deed was done. Mike was whisked out the door, into the ambulance and toward Oak Park hospital. Two of my friends went to the hospital with him. The officers had me sign their report, and they left. I called Mike's parents to inform them of the accident.

There were about twelve of us left. There was a strange silence in the apartment now. We stood around staring at each other in disbelief. On went the music. Slowly we all started to breath again. There was much to hash over for the next couple of hours. This truly was an event we'd never forget. Everyone promised that there would be no more karate exhibitions! Down went more beers. Out came the coke.

Soon it was time to make a coke run, and I was buying. For this deed, they would lavishly praise me for what a great guy I was, so off I went to the dealer. This would be how I'd live my life for the next seven years. Cocaine and liquor, with a few other drugs thrown in. It was a very comfortable pattern, until I realized that I couldn't stop, and that my brain was a neurological mess.

Cocaine use offers an intense, but short-lived euphoria. Over those seven years of increasing use I had more and more trouble dealing with the dreaded "coke comedown". Rather than face it full-on, I tired to blunt the effect with alcohol.

It is very difficult to describe what it's like to come off of a drug as powerful as cocaine. For me it was like experiencing all of the fears that life has to offer in a one-hour span. Then mix in the worst grief you've ever experienced and double it. This horrible experience does not always come to first time users or even those who have been at it for a year or two. But sooner or later, especially after years of increasing use, it's inevitable.

As the drug wore off, and I'd get that sense of quickly falling from nirvana, I'd crack a beer. Maybe it's counterintuitive, because alcohol is a depressant, but it seemed to help. Cocaine is an amphetamine, so I could go 24 or 48 hours without sleep, and it also allowed for mass consumption of alcohol. Thirty beers over a 24-hour period were not uncommon.

Sooner or later I'd have to crash – and crash I did. When I'd wake up that horrible cocaine low would be waiting for me. It didn't matter what time of day it was. If it was 7am, so be it, crack open a beer.

Why would I continue to do cocaine year in and year out if the comedowns were becoming unbearable? I didn't want to face my emotions. It's that simple. Any addiction is an avoidance of fears, anxiety, depression, worries, insecurities and all of the other psychic traumas we must face.

Chapter 11

-I always said he'd come to no good.
   Pink Floyd

"I Quit"

I was nicely settled in at Refco. I had a routine to follow every day and I as getting paid very well. The T-bond business in the south room had exploded. Our desk was producing incredible volume and had attracted an enormous group of new customers. We now had nine people working there, and I was the number two man right after Jerry, the guy who trained me. At 20-years-old, all the people under me were older. I knew that I was on my way to being rich. It would take about thirty seconds for it all to come crashing down.

***

I had an unforgettable encounter one night with Tom Dittmer, the owner of Refco. We were making vast amounts of money. So much so that it would vault Tom to the 225th wealthiest man in the country in 1981. He was very happy; so were we. Tom showed his appreciation of our work with generous bonuses, but on this night Tom showered me with a more important kind of bonus…praise. It happened during my second company trip to Las Vegas.

The first night there I was at the craps table in the Union Plaza. I didn't know much about craps, but it was simple enough to lay down money and pray. There were about five other people at the table with me. I heard "Hello Jim." from behind me. I turned to find Tom standing there with a smile on his face.

Tom stepped up to the table and plunked some chips down. He nabbed a waitress and asked her to bring a soft drink for himself and a Heineken for me. He started a conversation.

"So how do you and Jerry do it?" he asked as he placed a bet.

"Comin' out!" yelled the stick man. The player obediently rolled the dice.

I nervously ventured, "What do you mean, Tom?"
"I keep receiving calls from customers telling me how great you two are."

Before I could say anything, I noticed some 'higher ups' in Refco making their way to the table. It was like a scene out of "Night of the Living Dead". These pale VIP's were shuffling toward the table in a catatonic state droning in a monotone voice, "Tom's at the craps table. We must kiss his asssss."

When they got to the table they flanked Tom like secret service men. I realized he was still talking to me.

"You guys are doing a great job, and I just wanted to tell you thanks."

"My pleasure Tom. I appreciate the opportunity. It's great to work for Refco, and I like Jerry a lot." I gushed.

The drinks arrived. We toasted. For a brief moment I was in heaven, receiving such praise from Tom, a father figure in my world of trading. We talked back and forth for about six minutes before the brown-nosed zombies shoved me out of the way. A few minutes later

I had been pushed three people to the right of Tom, just another phone clerk among the traders.

* * *

Back in the south room, it was just a day like any other, with one exception. This would be my last day with Refco. My two and a half years with them was about to come to an abrupt end.

Jerry took a break at about 11:00 am. He told me he'd be back about 11:30, after he ate lunch. I asked Jerry if there was anything I should know or watch out for. He said no. This is where it all started, because it wasn't true.

What I didn't know was that Jerry's boss told him to leave me out of the loop. It was Jerry's bosses opinion that I was too young for the job and had a big mouth. He was reacting to the fact that I was on friendly terms with many of the clients. This same policy is why Tom was hearing good things about me. This is where the compliment came from. On the other hand, the powers working under him looked upon my behavior negatively. Why? Who knows. The bottom line is that I was not being told things that I needed to know. This day, I would pay with my job for being kept out of the loop.

When Jerry went on a break he didn't tell me that he was working an order for a big client that was placed early in the day. When the client placed the order the market price was at the order price, but the market moved off of that price quickly. So the client ended up buying only a portion of the bonds he wanted to buy at the specified price. When this happens the order stays in the trading pits with a broker in case the bond prices come back to the buy price. This is called "working the order." No one told me about this open order.

It just so happened that another client was also working an order at exactly the same price. As a matter of fact the order was for exactly the same quantity as well. The only thing that made those orders different was the account and order numbers on them. The bottom line was this: There were two orders in the pit with the broker to buy one hundred bonds at 85.10. (85.10 is the price the bonds were bought at.)

I got a call from one of the big clients on a particular line. Usually Jerry would answer this line, but he was on break. The client asked if he'd bought anything at 85.10. I told him I'd check.

I looked in the special area where we kept this clients' orders. The client was huge and he got exceptional service, including separating his orders from everyone else's. No other orders were supposed to be mixed in. I found an order at 85.10 and saw that forty-eight out of one hundred had been purchased. I assumed that this was his order – it was the right amount in the right place, and I hadn't been told about the other order.

I got back on the phone and told the client the news, thinking I was just confirming what he had already known. He hadn't known (since I was looking at the wrong order). He loved everybody at Refco, especially me. Those 48 bonds were worth $48,000 to him at the moment.

When Jerry came back from lunch, I told him how happy this big client was! Jerry stared at me in disbelief. He turned a bright shade of red.

"You didn't." He said, with fear in his eyes.

"Well, of course I did," I replied, wondering what was up. "It says he bought forty-eight on the order."

Jerry dropped his head.

"They aren't his."

Right then and there I knew it was all over for me at Refco. Tears started to well up in my eyes. In that split second, I could see everything that had happened, and all the events it took to get to this single moment in time.

Jerry explained that the bonds belonged to another client. There was no way we'd call back the client I talked to and tell him he couldn't have the bonds. There was no way we could tell the other client he couldn't have the bonds that were rightfully his. Refco would have to give forty-eight bonds to both clients, and Refco didn't own any bonds at 85.10. Refco would have to buy the bonds at the current price (which was much higher) from their error account. They would have to cut a check to the client for the difference. That difference was just over $48,000. I would have to pay for that 48k with my job.

I ran off the floor and headed to the stairwell just outside the south room to cry. A few minutes later, a security guard employed by the exchange approached me and asked if I was o.k. I nodded my head and uttered that I was. She told me to hang in there, and I sat for a little longer while I collected myself.

When I got back to Refco's trading desk in the south room, Jay was there. Jay was the head of both trading floors, and responsible for all of Refco's CBOT employees.

Jay had that 'I'm really pissed' face on. I couldn't bear the thought of Jay being angry with me. It was heart breaking, which was probably the worst of it all.

"What the fuck, Jim?" Jay said, holding the order in his hand.

"Jay, I'm so sorry," I barely muttered, choking back tears.

"You know we have to make this good," he said to me.

I just nodded. Jay and Jerry talked back and forth for a while, and then Jay walked away. For now I would have to stay at the desk and work for the next two hours, waiting for the market to close at 2:00 pm. Then I'd find out the consequences of the blunder. It was the longest two hours of my life.

The ruling came down later that afternoon. When I got to the office to complete my afternoon duties, the assistant floor manager, from the grain room, was waiting for me. Jerry was there too.

"We do not want to fire you, because you're good at what you do, and we don't want to lose you." Said the assistant floor manager.

The assistant floor manager was one of the biggest jerks I had met in my life. We were both hot heads and stubborn, so we didn't get along. My immaturity didn't help. He told me about the decision in the most condescending way he could. He had me, and he knew it. He loved shoving mistakes in your face, then rubbing it in with as much cruelty as he could.

"You will be taken out of the bond room and work in the grain room with me. I'll be your boss, and I'm going to scrutinize every thing you do. Don't think for a second you'll have the freedom in the grains that you had in the bonds. Because, if you make a 48k mistake in the grains, I will kick your ass. Count on it. You will answer the phones at the meal and oil desk. Your afternoon duties will change also. You will no longer work on the bond out-trades. You will work on the meal and oil out-trades." He finished with glee.

This was the last thing I wanted. I knew the grains were *not* the place to be, and the meal and oil desk was the slowest desk on the floor. I had no desire to work on anything that didn't have to do with bonds.
I said, "Fine." I asked to speak to Jerry alone. The assistant floor manager left.

When the door closed, I couldn't contain my sadness. Jerry recoiled in his chair and said, "Jim I do not want to see you cry."

I interrupted saying that bonds were my life. I didn't want be taken out of the south room, but Jerry said it was out of his hands. It was a gargantuan mistake, and I'd pissed off a lot of people at Refco – people who spent their afternoon putting out fires because of me.

I lowered my head, stood up and thanked Jerry. I walked into Jay's boss's office down the hall and asked if I could talk with him. He said yes and began to blurt out exactly what he thought of me.

"You fucking morons on the floor," he started. "You fucking idiots think you can come into this industry without any college education and take the world by the balls? You guys are stupid."

I stood up and thanked him for his advice and said, "I quit."

Chapter 12

-You slip out of your depth and out of your mind
With your fear flowing out behind you
As you claw the thin ice.
     Pink Floyd

"Two Steps Backward"

It was strange not having anywhere to be on Monday morning. My routine had changed abruptly, and I really didn't care. Well, at least I pretended I didn't care. That's how I was raised. Forget about it and move on. Don't feel the pain. It's too much to bear.

I think my parents were more in a panic than I was. Since I would no longer be receiving a paycheck and had spent most of my money on blow, I would have to move back to their house. I'm sure they were not thrilled about this. After raising six children, they'd had their fill of problems. What could be worse for them then to have finally gotten rid of us, only to have me straggle back? Add to this that I was also the only child without a college education. They must have been going nuts behind closed doors.

So home I went, storing all of my possessions in the basement of my parents' house. Fine with me, it was time to party. This is how I was learning to deal with the pain. I'd love to tell you about the partying I did for the next few months, if I could only remember it. Most of those days are an alcoholic and drug induced blur. One memory does remain though, my first serious attempt at suicide.

What leads a person to suicide? Many things, I guess – a kind of desperation that arises from hopelessness perhaps – the end result of a cascade of influences. The thing is, this loss of hope can be needless. It can be depression talking. Life can seem hopeless when it is not - when hope is there, just for the asking.

In my case it was a cascade of events made worse by a family predisposition to depression and alcohol use.

Where once I had a job, money and independence, I now had no job, no money, and was living once again with my parents. My girlfriend broke up with me. I had no education. Things looked grim and drinking was what I knew. It's what I saw as the answer to all problems. This was something I'd picked up early on. When I was growing up, most of the adults around me drank – especially when there were problems. So I'd cope by sedating myself. I had the perfect excuse to binge.

The problem is that we can't escape depression by sedating ourselves with alcohol. Alcohol is a depressant. It can only lead to deeper depression. The stress from losing my job, independence and the girl I'd been dating at the time, with the addition of heavy drinking, was a depression cocktail.

The more I drank, the more I slipped into despair. The more I slipped into despair, the more I saw no way out. The more I saw no way out the more I drank.

After living back at home for about six weeks, my mother pulled me aside and asked me what I was going to do with my life.

"Probably go back down to the board of trade and look for another job," I said to appease her.

"Excellent!" She said, and left it at that.

The next morning, my year-old niece would single handedly stop me from killing myself.

When I woke up that morning I was hung over and depressed. My mind was reeling from conflicting thoughts. On one side, I heard the fearless problem solver who never gives up and never slows down. This side of me knew that I could be successful, but only if I took myself to the limit. It said, "Get out there and kick some ass!" The other side told me that I was fat, ugly, stupid, worthless, self-centered, smoked too much and would never amount to anything. There was only one way I knew how to shut down the noise in my head - drink, but that wasn't making anything better either. My perspective was narrowed by age, depression and substance abuse. To me it looked like there was no hope, and I saw no other alternative than death.

The house was empty. I headed to the bathroom. The razor blades stared at me from the medicine cabinet, begging me. Such a small instrument, I thought, with such a deadly consequence. I grabbed the blades and withdrew one. Tears flooded my eyes as I began hacking at my wrist, producing an enormous amount of blood. Of course, I did it over the sink to keep from making a mess!

One wrist done, I started on the other, but suddenly heard the front door open. The house was very old, and the front door was a massive piece of oak. When it opened the sound could not be mistaken for anything else. Then the voice of my little niece came traveling from the front hall, up the stairs and into my ears. She was pure joy. Her voice carried that joy to me. I sank down to the floor, convulsing with heavy sobs.

"What am I doing?" I cried to myself. "Just listen to that little voice. I'll never hear it again, or be with her again if I continue this."
I heard my sister-in-law call out, "Anybody home?"

I waited for a few moments to answer, trying to make my decision.

Finally I said, "I am."

I cleaned up the blood, threw away the blade and tried to stop the bleeding with a towel. I slowly walked downstairs and told my sister-in-law Jeanne that I needed help. Looking down at my niece, I knew that I'd made the right decision. Jeanne got on the phone and called my Mom at work. After assessing the wounds, we decided that it was best not to go to the hospital for fear of getting the system involved. My mom would call and make an appointment with a psychologist. I agreed.

This was my second visit to the psychologist. I was 15 when I went the first time. My parents decided to run a battery of tests on me at a psychiatric hospital to see if I was normal. I was flunking out of high school, spending every waking moment at my girlfriend's house and I was breaking the law left and right. My parents were just trying to help.

The tests showed that I was "normal", whatever that means, but it was decided that I should have someone to talk to about my problems; hence, the psychologist.

By the time I was 15 whenever anyone wanted to know how I was doing I automatically responded that I was fine. When I saw the psychologist, that's what I told him. We had two sessions and I pronounced myself cured.

Five years later, I was back. This time his advice was to do everything in my power to get back on the trading floor. Get a job no matter what the job was. It doesn't matter if it's a runner's job.

The psychologist was trying to get some structure in my life. Sitting at home brooding wasn't the answer. He knew I liked the CBOT because I talked about it in length with him. He also new that I had created some self worth within myself because of the CBOT. Going back to the CBOT seemed logical to him.

But getting a runners job? *That* statement hit me hard. The thought of getting a runner's job was too much. I was a *phone clerk* and an *out-trade checker*! I imagined myself back on the trading floor as a runner. It would be embarrassing! How could I possibly lift my head up again?

In the end, it made sense to me. Back then I didn't know why. My gut told me to trust him. I went down to the CBOT in search of a runner's job. I would try to get a phone clerk position, but agreed to all involved that if a runner's job came up, I'd snag it.

Chapter 13

-Waiting for the winds of change
To sweep the clouds away.
    Rush

"I'm Back"

My job hunt was short-lived. The first office I walked into offered me a job as a runner. A big blow to my ego, but I had made an agreement and would stick by it.

The following day, I began working for Maduff in the bond room as a runner. They were taking a chance by hiring me because they knew I was over-qualified. I reassured them that I wouldn't up and quit on them, knowing the second I hit the floor I'd start shopping myself around for a phone clerk's job. I also knew I'd give Maduff my best effort while I worked for them. I was starting over.

Maduff's trading desk was on the opposite side of the south room from Refco's desk, which I avoided like the plague. To this day, I can vividly remember what it was like that first day back. My stomach churned with shame and regret. I feared running into one of my old Refco buddies. I carried all these feelings like fifty-pound weights. The hours ticked by painfully slowly.

There were a couple of silver linings though. One silver lining was the people who worked on the floor for Maduff, especially Mike and Michelle. Mike was a runner, and Michelle was our boss. She was very nice, and I came to respect her immediately. Mike and I remained great friends until the day I left the CBOT for good.

The other was, it was an exciting to be in the Chicago financial district. In the few months that I was away from the CBOT, more bodies had somehow been crammed into the pit and the surrounding desks. This was a result of the astronomical volume the bonds were doing. In 1981, the bonds became the most actively traded commodity in the world. The fire department must have been very uneasy about the situation. If a fire broke out, it wouldn't have been pretty.

The south room was becoming a sauna, too. Fans were stationed at both entrances of the south room and the CBOT ended up cutting a huge hole in the wall behind Maduff's desk to try to get some air circulating in the room.

There was a gigantic metal grate in the hole and I could look through the slats in the grating and watch the construction of the new building the CBOT was constructing next door.

***

Construction on the new CBOT building began in late 1980. It opened in 1982. It is 23 stories high and it features a stunning 12-story high atrium.

During this same period the Chicago Board Options Exchange (CBOE), began construction on a new building directly south of the CBOT. It opened on February 21, 1984. When the new option building is combined with the CBOT, it creates a massive financial trading center and impressive trading floors. The options floor covers 45,000 sq. ft. (The new grain floor, 32,000 sq. ft.; the new financial floor, 19,000 sq.

ft.) The south room at the CBOT, which was now reserved for later use, was 5,000 Sq. Ft. by comparison. Included in this massive complex is the Chicago Stock Exchange, which moved to its new trading floor to the south end of the options building.

***

As I stared through this hole in the wall and heard the workers hammering, sawing and nailing together the new grain floor, I wasn't thinking of the new building or the politics of the CBOT. I was thinking about how I was going to get into the bond pit and trade.

At the time it seemed like the best way into the pit was through a company like Refco, Merrill Lynch, Smith Barney, or like Donaldson, Lufkin and Jenrette (DLJ). Their trading desk was right by Maduff's. I learned that the boss at the DLJ desk was Tim Anderson.

I began to pursue a phone clerk job with Tim just weeks after starting at Maduff. Tim was a tall, thin, slightly balding man. His enthusiasm for life was exhilarating. He would become yet another father figure at the CBOT.

DLJ was looking to hire a new phone clerk as they expanded their trading operations. My target date to get them to hire me was the opening of the new financial trading floor in April of 1982. Day after day I hounded Tim to give me an answer. Psychologically, the anticipation was excruciating. Finally the answer came. Tim said that I could begin working for them the day the new trading floor opened.

I was back!

Chapter 14

-All the busy little creatures,
 Chasing out their destinies.
        Rush

"The New Floor"

On April 19, 1982, the new financial trading floor opened on what was once the grain floor, and I started my new job with DLJ as a phone clerk and out-trade checker.

As I learned the ropes I became friends with my co-workers. DLJ was not a small company, but their trading operation on the bond floor was. There were only four of us, Tim, Michael, Shannon and myself. Our boss was Taylor Hurst. Taylor spent most of his time working off of the trading floor. I couldn't have landed with a better group of people. I learned so much from them.

Michael taught me the value of conduct inside and outside of the workplace. He also taught me professionalism. He taught me that it was O.K. to have fun outside of work but to always conduct myself like a gentleman no matter where I was.

Shannon taught me that work was not everything. Sure, it was important to do a great job at work, but it could be done without getting wrapped up in every detail. It was just fine to let go of work when you left for the day.

Tim was also in a new position with DLJ. He'd just entered the trading pit as a house broker. Tim's move up would lead to my introduction to *Broker Assisting,* a huge step towards my goal of securing my first membership on the CBOT.

Tim's boss was Taylor Hurst. The two of them are without a doubt a couple of the greatest people I've ever met. Tim and Taylor had very similar managing styles. They were both great listeners and both great leaders. Both knew how to motivate, and each had a genuine concern about the well-being of those working for them. They wanted us to work hard, but they wanted us happy.

I was privileged enough to get to know Taylor outside the CBOT. I'll never forget the spring of 1982, shortly after I started working for DLJ. I was telling Taylor how excited I was about the NCAA championship on TV that evening. He ended up coming over to my apartment and brought the beer! Special Export no less! How cool was that? We had a great time. Taylor was excited to see my new apartment - and to meet my new bride-to-be.

***

Since I was back in the workplace and earning good money, it was time to move out of my parents' house again. This move would be my last. I had a very different motivation this time. Through some mutual friends, I had met my soul mate.

These new buddies kept telling me about this friend of theirs, Diana. They said over and over that I had to meet her. Finally I did, on April 30th 1982 and we connected immediately.

Well, I should say that she connected with me first, by backing her car into my right knee! After I got in the back seat of her car, I gladly accepted her apology. I needed to stretch out my leg. It was killing me, so I propped it between the driver's and passenger's seat and ended up crushing her favorite cassette tape in the process. I apologized. Luckily, she accepted and we called a truce. That night we fell in love, and we moved in together within three months.

Our new apartment was back in Forest Park, right above the bar my buddy owned. Yes, the same guy I rented my second apartment from. It was big, very modern, had skylights and it was newly redecorated. But most important, it was above a bar. That suited me fine. I was drinking like a fish by then.

***

Let's take a closer look at how brokers do business. This will be necessary if you are going to understand what I was trying to get myself into.

There were two types of traders on the trading floor, *brokers* and *locals* (a.k.a. *market makers*). Brokers make their money by executing orders for their clients, trading houses (a.k.a. brokerage houses and clearing houses, but they're all one in the same). Locals make their money by trading their own money. I'd roughly estimate that for every broker in the bond pit in 1982, there were ten locals.

A broker buys or leases a seat on the exchange. This gives him or her the right to enter certain pits and trade certain commodities on the exchange. To get customers, they must establish themselves in the trading pit.

There are several was to get started as a broker. You can know someone already established and ask for help. You can work your way up through an already existing independent trading operation, or you could work you way up at a brokerage house like DLJ, and then become a house broker.

After becoming a house broker, you could leave and become established as an independent broker. Independent brokers worked for themselves and paid their own employees. Independents would try to get business from the trading houses, like DLJ. Trading houses were often happy to have an independent execute its orders. By using an independent broker, the trading house shifted all the risk of errors and out-trades onto the independent. Employee overhead was also shifted to the independent. Trading houses would pay the independent broker a commission to execute the order at the best possible price and that was it – no muss, no fuss.

The rapid increase in the volume of bond trading during the early Eighties created new pressures on the system. In response, something new was catching fire among the trading pit brokers - the hiring of *Broker Assistants*.

When I first started at DLJ, Tim worked the pit as a house broker. Shannon, Michael or I would work the phones and hand signal the orders to Tim in the pit, but there was a problem with this system. Once we signaled to Tim and he turned around to execute the trade in the pit, he was unavailable to us. Seconds count in the world of commodities. The markets move as quickly as lightning, with millions of dollars changing hands every second. What if the trading customer suddenly wanted to change his order? And what if it was impossible to get Tim's attention because his back was to us?

The answer to this problem was to get Tim a Broker Assistant. That Broker Assistant would be me.

Brokers and their assistants stood on the top step of the trading pit. The reason for this was to allow their assistants to be the voice of the broker back at the trading desk. Assistants would face away from the broker and look to the companies' trading desks, which surround the pit. The assistants job was to immediately communicate transactions in the pit to the trading desks via hand signals. They would indicate to the desk exactly who was buying and selling and at what price the market was trading. They would also take orders from the desks and give them to the broker verbally for execution in the pit. Then, the assistant would hand signal back to the desks exactly what price they executed the order.

With broker assistants now handling the communication back and forth from the desk, the broker was freed to watch the action in the trading pit.

Hand signals are the lifeblood of communication between the broker's operation in the pit and his clients at the trading desk. That flow of communication enabled the trading desks to tell their office traders exactly what was happening in the bond pit. Those hand signals flowing from the Broker Assistant's hands to the phone clerk were a vital link to providing great service. A good Broker Assistant was key to success. The speed and quality of this communication could literally make or break a broker.

That's where my dexterity paid off. My fingers could move individually like lightning, like the fingers of a jazz pianist!

Chapter 15

-When I heard that he was gone,
I felt a shadow cross my heart.
　　Rush

"Shannon's Wave"

My heart was beating furiously. Tim had taken me aside, after the close, to inform me of my new duties.

"What about going in the pit and broker assisting for me?" He asked.

"Gee. Can I have some time to think it over, Tim?" I kidded. "OK, that's enough time. I accept!"

"Great, Monday you're in the pit with me."

I'd experienced many opening bells in the CBOT in the prior two and half years. Now, for the first time, I would experience the opening bell from the trading pit. I would be contributing to the workings of the pit. To say that I was excited is huge understatement.

My first day working for Tim in the bond pit was nothing less than spectacular. Shannon and Michael were working the phones and anticipating the market's open. I asked Tim to give me the opening call, that is, at what price he thought the bonds were going to open at. He told me and I relayed my first hand signal from the pit to a trading desk.

When the bell rang, chills ran up my spine. I was here! I was a part of the trading pit!

I began hand signaling (flashing) the trading price to the desk. Then I relayed which company(s) or big locals were buying and selling. In turn, Shannon and Michael would relay all this information, to the office trader on the other end of the phone. Then I flashed the market size – and on and on.

This was my new job – to constantly flash all of this information. I was excellent at it from the beginning, and I would only get better. Other brokers in the pit began to take notice. Soon, they would be interested in luring me away from DLJ.

Tim and I became good friends. He was more a mentor to me than a boss. He could see my immaturity and helped me draw boundaries when I was overzealous, which was often. I pushed boundaries because I didn't now any better. Tim, Michael and Shannon were patient and very understanding with me. Somehow they saw through my antics to my potential. They saw an excellent broker assistant, and they truly wanted to see me succeed. For that I'm very grateful. Nine months later everything changed.

* * *

Most of the time Tim executed our orders, and sometimes Michael would execute them. Sometimes, when neither could be in the pit for some reason, I'd stay in the pit and give the orders to an independent broker. That's what I was doing on Friday, January 14th 1983. Michael wasn't there, and Tim hadn't shown up that morning, which was odd.

There wasn't much trading activity that day. Shannon was at the trading desk. I saw her pick up the phone, and I began to flash the market, but she waved me off. Apparently it wasn't a customer on the other end of the line. After a moment Shannon looked up and waved me over to the desk. I asked her what she wanted, and she waved to me more urgently. I was struck by the look on her face. As I walked up to the desk I could see the tears streaming down her face.

"Timmy's dead." She said to me as she hung up the phone.

"What?" I said in utter disbelief.

Shannon said that Tim had died of a heart attack the previous night.

She explained that Tim had been found dead in his apartment.

I wandered back to the trading pit. I reported the news to the others. The news spread quickly.

Tim died from a massive ingestion of cocaine. His heart gave out. I didn't know he was using cocaine on a regular bases at the time of his death. I'd only learn of this months later. The cause of his death didn't stop me from using coke in the following years. My thinking was, that it couldn't happen to me.

Why would someone who was so successful, good looking and basically seemed to have life by the balls use cocaine? As my career progressed in the trading pits over the next few years, I got my answer. The stress of being a trader was immense.

was the first time as an adult that someone close to me died. I guess shock set in immediately. I don't know. What I remember is becoming numb.

When Tim died, it was if my own father had passed. He was one of the many father figures I sought out in the CBOT. I looked up to Tim and he treated me like a son. I felt lost and desperate after he was gone.

At the time I wasn't aware that Tim was a father figure. Without thinking, I found myself dropping by my parents house more often. I needed to know that everything would be okay. Unfortunately, when I tried to connect with my real Father, I was rejected. My father's way of handling death was to ignore his emotions. He'd numb himself with alcohol so he didn't have to deal with the pain. When I tried to express my sadness over Tim's death, he would become very uncomfortable and spurt out meaningless statements about how he was sorry I lost Tim, blah blah blah. Statements that were not connected to his emotions but connected to his unfeeling brain. Useless thoughts. Thoughts that did me absolutely no good. Because I am feeler. My feelings needed guidance and my Father was not willing to deal with his own emotions, let alone help me with mine. This was the ultimate rejection.

The tradition of not feeling was being passed down to me by my Dad. He received it from his Dad, etc. I was learning not to feel so I didn't want to grieve Tim, and I didn't want to touch that other pain deep inside – the hole in my soul that represented a true *feeling* relationship with my real father. The loss of Tim and further rejection from my Father was too much. The result was to turn to drinking. Exactly how my Dad would have dealt with it.

Shannon and I stayed the rest of the day until the market closed at 2:00 pm. I will never understand why DLJ didn't close their trading desk for the rest of the day. The market was slow. The biggest trader at DLJ stopped trading after learning the news of Tim's passing. There was nothing to do. It was a long and emotional wait for the 2:00 pm bell. Finally, it rang, and I headed home, my emotions in turmoil.

By Monday plans had been made for a wake and the funeral. Finally, at the wake, I would cry deep, painful tears. Rarely in my life have I felt such deep grief. Thankfully, Diana was there to comfort me.

With Tim's passing, things would take a dramatic turn in my career. An unexpected mentor would lead me to what would become my final stop in the CBOT before entering the application for my seat.

Chapter 16

-Into the distance, a ribbon of black
Stretched to the point of no turning back
　　Pink Floyd

"Bob"

Time passed slowly the next few months. I recovered from Tim's death as best I could by concentrating on being the best broker assistant in the pit.

We began using several different independent brokers to execute our orders. One of them was Bob Laser, or 'Laz' (pronounced 'Laze') for short.

One day, just after the closing bell rang, Michael asked to talk with me. We walked over to the empty trading pit on the southeast side of the floor and sat on the top step.

Michael began, "Bob Laser asked me if you would be interested in coming to work for him. He talked with me first, because he didn't want to take you away from us and create any problems. I think this would be a very good move for you, Jim."

"Sounds good, but I've always worked for trading companies. I don't know about working for an independent broker."

"True. However, if you're to reach your goal of becoming a trader in the pit, this is the best opportunity you'll have."

"So there's not much of a chance of DLJ getting me a seat?"

"I'm sure that will happen down the road. But, with Laz you'll probably get it quicker and have a better chance for success."

I thanked Michael and told him that I'd talk with Bob in the morning.

I approached Bob before the opening of the market, while he was clearing up his out-trades.

"What's up, Bob?" I asked.

"Are you interested in coming to work for me?"
"As your broker assistant?"
"Yes." I didn't hold back one iota with my next statement. "When can I get my seat?"

Bob laughed, "One thing at a time. I cannot promise you anything, but if things go well, and I get more business, then we'll talk in a year."

My heart leapt to my throat. A year? This was unbelievable! I was so close to my membership on the CBOT now that I could taste it.

I held out my hand to seal the deal and told him, "I accept."

Bob would, without a doubt, become one of the greatest father figures in my life. I would constantly seek his approval over the years we would spend together in the CBOT. I wanted him to acknowledge my accomplishments with a pat on the back. I wanted him to encourage me when I was feeling down.

I wanted him to stick up for me when another person wronged me. I wanted him to fill the void my own father had left.

Over the years I spent with Bob, I came to realize that I was asking for something he couldn't give me; a father-son relationship. He couldn't give that to me because he was my boss, not my father. He didn't hire me to be his son, he hired me to be his employee. An employee who was there to perform a specific task. The void still existed.

I would leave DLJ and begin working for Laz in one week with thanks going to Michael, my unexpected mentor. Back then I didn't know that he was guiding me to what was best for me, career wise. Michael knew I wasn't corporate material so he steered me towards what I did best, which was working in the pit.

* * *

In Bob's trading operation, there was another broker assistant, a trade checker and myself, for a total of three employees. Bob also worked with another independent broker, Doug, and they'd cover for each other when one had to leave the pit. Doug stood directly to Bob's left. Doug also had a trading operation with the same number of employees.

Bob had several clients he executed orders for. Now I was watching three trading desks at a time and sometimes four. I was flashing fast and furiously every second of every day.

The bond market was quickly gaining momentum. Bob was doing more and more business. It was very exciting. But this excitement came with a price. Again, I was moving up the CBOT ladder. My career was advancing at a very fast pace. I didn't realize that with more responsibility comes more pressure, and because I didn't know how to deal with that pressure, I turned to what I knew – alcohol and drugs.

I was drinking after work to sooth myself and calm down. During the day, I needed the boost of amphetamines to keep myself going. Weekends would consist of drinking beer and gin and snorting cocaine. I could begin as early as noon on a Saturday and by 7:00 pm I was at my coke dealer's house.

The drug and alcohol abuse happened gradually. It crept up on me. I didn't really realize what I was doing to myself. At each moment I just reacted in the only way I knew how, and tried to keep up the pace. Bob was paying me extremely well. So monetarily at least, I could afford my lifestyle.

Diana and I were to marry in June, 1983. The responsibility of marriage added to my job-related stress. It was all beginning to take a toll on me physically and psychologically, and I didn't have a clue. Predictably, my drinking would begin to interfere with my job for the first time in my life. Laz laid down the law the first time I showed up late for work, saying it was unacceptable. I would take his talk to heart, well, for a month or so anyway.

During the following eight months made some employee changes that lead to the hiring of a new broker assistant named Jerry Keeley. Jerry and I knew each other from high school. We became a phenomenal tag team. We also became close friends.

Soon it would be Christmas, 1983. Bob and Doug took their employees and spouses to dinner in the city to thank us for a great year. They'd also hand out Christmas bonuses. I received a check from Bob for $5,000, and Doug gave me $1,000. I was stunned at the size of those checks. I didn't think I would ever have to worry about money again.

Chapter 17

-Polarize me, Sensitize me, Criticize me, Civilize me, Compensate me, Animate me, Complicate me, Elevate me.
      Rush

"ING"

We entered 1984, breaking all kinds of volume records in the trading pit. Bob's trading operation was expanding, and he needed relief from trading. Standing in the trading pit, day after day, was wearing on him. The logical step for Bob was to have me take over for him in the pit, so that he could get out once in a while.

At about the same time the CBOT, for various growth-related reasons, came out with a new rule: if a broker in the bond pit had a broker assistant who was going to stand on the top step of the trading pit, then that assistant must have a membership. The brokers needed to have their broker assistants stand on the top step of the pit for the best visibility, and so that they could communicate orders to the broker and transactions to the desk. Brokers were put in a position where they had to either buy or lease a membership for their assistant(s) to us.

It was evident that it was time for my application to be entered for membership on the Chicago Board of Trade.

In May of 1984, I entered my application for membership with the secretary's office in the CBOT.

Ahead of me was a two-month process before I could receive that ultimate ticket.

First, there would be an announcement of all applicants that applied that month in the monthly newsletter that went out to all members. That way, if someone had an objection they could raise their concerns with the membership committee. No one objected.

Then, there'd be the exam - a monster of a test, (Back then it was the "Series 3") that spanned three hours. I needed 75% to get a passing grade on the exam. I was worried. You may recall my poor academics in high school. I wasn't a test taker and never would be. When I set my mind on something though, I usually did okay. Even in my sedated state I knew I'd do whatever it took to pass.

After the exam there'd be "Simulated Trading". I wasn't worried about the simulated trading because it wasn't a test. It was there so that a future member could get the feel for actual trading.

Then, I'd finish with the signing of 'The Book,' which resides in the secretary's office in the CBOT. Every member that ever traded at the CBOT had signed that book. The signing of the book was just a formality, so the only serious hoop was the exam.

If all went well, I'd receive my membership. The next two months would be anxious ones, yet exciting for me.

I studied the best I could and entered the testing room on a Friday afternoon, armed with my No. 2 pencil and, thankfully, a calculator. It was brutal.

Even though I wouldn't be trading options, it was a part of the exam, and it was twice as hard as the rest. I struggled with one question that had six parts to it. Over and over I fingered the numbers into the calculator. I'd done pretty well on other parts of the exam. I figured that maybe I missed twenty questions out of the hundred asked. Even so, that left me in a precarious position. If I missed this six-part question, I'd probably get a 74 - not good enough – more numbers punched in, more calculations made. Time was running out. Finally, I had a breakthrough and logged what I thought was the right answer.

I turned in the exam after sitting for over two and a half hours of the three hours allotted. Now, I'd sweat until Monday to find out the results.

When Monday came, I was tense. At about 10:00 am, I left the trading pit and found a phone. I called the number for test results.

"Name please," the voice said on the other end.

"James Goulding."

"80. Congratulations."

"Thank you!" I smiled the biggest smile I ever had, and hung up.

* * *

On July 9, 1984, I signed the members' book in the secretary's office signifying my official status as a member of the Chicago Board of Trade. The only thing left was to go to the third floor and get my badge.

When I entered the office where the badges were made, I was greeted by a smiling woman who ushered me to a table.

She asked me what acronym I wanted to go on my badge. (The 'badge' represents the actual 'Seat' on the exchange and is pinned to your trading jacket so other traders in the pit can identify you.)

I said JAG for my initials…James <u>A</u>llen <u>G</u>oulding. She flipped through a computer printout, scanning the names and acronyms of all the members.

"That's taken." she said.

"How about JG?" I said.

Flip, scan.

"That's taken, too. "Let's see…What's your name again?"

"James Allen Goulding."

"What about ING?" she offered.

"Bingo!" I exclaimed.

My picture was taken, the badge assembled. She handed me the final product. I thanked her, pinned it on my trading jacket and walked out into the hallway on my way to the trading floor.

I stepped onto the escalator and headed up, feeling pride like I had never felt before. As I walked on the floor, the guys in Bob's trading operation caught site of me and leaned out of the pit, craning their necks to see if *it* was pinned on my trading jacket.

I floated up the trading steps to my broker assistant's position and began to flash the market to our customers. Bob turned around and congratulated me, then Doug, then some of the other traders. Then my customers took notice and silently applauded. I was beaming.

I couldn't help but to think back to the first opening bell I'd experienced, watching the pandemonium in the pit. Running my first order into the corn pit. Getting promoted to phone clerk then losing my job at Refco. There was the suicide attempt, and then coming back, swallowing my pride. Starting at DLJ. Broker assisting for the first time, and then Tim's death. The memories washed over me. I was now standing on the top step of the pit, I was twenty-two-years-old and I was "ING".

Later that day I called Mom. She was nothing less than elated and sent the information blazing through the family tree as soon as we hung up.

I went by to see my parents later that evening. The adulation I most wanted was from my father. On my way there I envisioned him jumping up from his chair and embracing me, giving me hearty pats on the back, and smiling ear to ear. I could see him in my mind's eye strutting as proudly as a peacock. I could hear him saying, "My son! The Broker! What a success! He did this all on his own! I'm so proud of him. He overcame such adversity!"

His real reaction was quite different from the one I imagined. It was muted. He half-smiled. There was no "Way to go!", no "I'm proud of you!". Nothing.

Dad was so proud of me when I was promoted from a runner to a phone clerk. How could he not be LIT UP over this? To say the least, I was confused. "Oh well." I thought; "He'll really be proud of me when I make my first million!"

Chapter 18

-We have taken care of everything
The words you hear, the songs you sing
The pictures that give pleasure to you eyes.
    Rush

"Trading"

I was now an official member of the Chicago Board of Trade and that gave me the right to trade. The beauty of this was that now I had two new income streams, besides what Bob was paying me. The first was the money I could earn as a broker, and the second was trading as a local.

* * *

What are the traders doing in the pit? The traders are simply buying and selling a commodity. What's a commodity? Something that can be bought, sold, traded and speculated on, just like corn. My commodity was T-Bonds, so I will explain my work from that angle.

Treasury bonds are fully-backed U.S. debt instruments. They have maturities of more than one year and pay the investor a fixed annual rate of return or coupon which is paid semi-annually. The return on a Treasury note or bond is equal to its face value times the coupon interest rate. They can be traded just like corn.

For a trade to be completed there must be a buyer and seller agreeing on a price for the commodity that they are trading. Traders are looking for people to match what they want to do – buy, sell and trade at a specific price. A broker will get an order to buy or sell at a given price, and they often get these orders as the market hits the price the customers want – but that price can change at any moment. What makes things interesting is that commodity prices are a moving target.

The way they tell other traders in the pit what they are doing is by using hand signals and shouting what price and how many contracts they are trying to do.

When you see the traders jumping up and down and shouting on TV, the market is trading their price somewhere in the pit, and they want to either get the other traders' attention, or just let everyone in the pit know that they have bonds at the price the market is trading – just in case some is buying. When the market is actively trading a certain price and the market changes to a new price, that's when there is a great deal of activity in the pit. When there are three hundred people doing that, it appears to be pandemonium. It's not. It's just buyers and sellers agreeing on the same price.

That's why they call it 'Open out-cry'. Traders are literally yelling and crying out loud in the open where everyone can see.

***

As a broker, I'd earn a $1.25 for every contract I executed in the pit. I began to execute orders that first day. Bob limited me to orders that were one to five contracts in size. If I filled an order that was five contracts in size ("5-Lot"), then I'd rack up a commission of $6.25.

I was also allowed to trade as a local, risking my own money. In order to do this I had to open an account at

TransMarket Group, which was a brokerage house at the CBOT. They allowed me to open an account and trade because Bob backed me. Put another way, Bob put his ass on the line. If I had a big out-trade or error, Bob said he'd cover my losses if I couldn't.

On that very first day I traded some of my own money for the first time. In fact, two of the other locals gave me winning trades. It was a ritual in the trading pit. The locals would buy and sell a 1-lot at a loss to themselves and at a profit to a new trader. A couple of locals each gave me winning trades, and I made a profit of $62.50, minus a small commission that went to TransMarket and the CBOT.

The first order I filled for a customer that day was a "1-lot" buy order for one of Bob's clients. They told me to "Buy one bond at the market." Simply put, they wanted the best possible price at that particular moment for one bond. The market at the moment was fifteen bid at sixteen offered. The customer assumed they'd pay no more than sixteen. It was a given with such a small order. I knew this so, before I turned to execute the order, I told the customer to expect no worse than sixteen. Then I turned to the traders and tried to execute my first trade in the pit.

I bid, "15 for 1 - 15 for 1."

The other traders wanted to sell at sixteen. They said to my bid, "Sell it at 16."

Before I could respond the market suddenly moved to sixteen, bid. I bid sixteen for one and the locals said, "Sell it at 17."

In other words I had promised sixteen, the market had gone higher, and I hadn't bought anything yet.

The difference between the price of sixteen and seventeen on a one-lot order was $31.25. If I bought the order at seventeen, then I'd have to give a check to the customer for $31.25, because I'd promised sixteen. If I filled the order at seventeen and had to give the customer a check for $31.25 and the customer was paying me a commission of $1.25, that wouldn't be very profitable. This illustrates the risk a broker takes when filling orders in the pit.

The market was sixteen, bid at seventeen. Before I could respond the market moved to seventeen, bid. In about 4 seconds, it rose to twenty, bid. I still hadn't bought the 1-lot. If I bought it at twenty, I'd owe the customer "four tics" or 4 x $31.25 = $125.00 – for a commission of $1.25.

I finally filled the order at twenty, but the local on the other side of the trade changed the price for me to nineteen. That was great, but I still had to tell the customer that I filled the order at nineteen instead of sixteen. The customer stared at me, laughed and said, "Cut us a check."

The results of that first day are as follows: I made $62.50 trading my own money and executed nineteen contracts for a total of $23.50 in brokerage. However I had to cut a check to a customer for $125. That made my first day a net loss. Welcome to the life of a broker.

The days of summer wore on, and I started executing more and more orders. Bob began taking breaks by the end of the summer, and I would step up to the front row of the pit and execute orders. Bob's customers gained confidence in me and allowed me to fill bigger and bigger orders. By the middle of December, I'd racked up over $20,000 worth of commissions and made another $1,000 trading on my own money. $21,000 in just over five months, plus salary. Not bad for a guy with a high school education.

* * *

Diana and I had moved to a new apartment in early 1986 on Oak Park Avenue, in Oak Park. It was a big Oak Park house that had been converted into three apartments, very large and newly decorated. We lived on the first floor of the house. The owners lived upstairs, and another couple lived in the remaining apartment that was also upstairs.

This place would abet in escalating my drinking and drug intake. The people who lived in the complex partied, big time. I didn't think it could be done, but I had no idea just how bad I could get. Am I saying that it was the fault of the people who lived there? No. We seek out those who have the same beliefs as we do. If we are on a health kick, we will attract healthy people. If our passion is dancing, we find other dancers or they find us. I was into numbing myself to the extreme; hence, I found the same type of people.

***

In 1986 I began executing more and more orders. I was averaging about $25,000 a month by March. This was an astronomical increase in just a few months. Remember, in my first six months of executing trades I did $20,000 in business. Now I was doing that, and more, every month. With these kinds of returns, Bob soon passed two of his employee's salaries onto me and stopped paying me a salary. I was now an independent broker with my own employees, and I had just turned 24-years-old.

Bob bought the seat that I was using to trade with in 1985. In July of 1986 I bought the seat from Bob; I was now a seat owner. This was a monumental occasion for me. I hand delivered the check to Bob while he was in the pit. Then I said, "See ya!"

"Where are you going?"
"Where else? To the bar."

It was 9:00 am.

My advancement to broker came with all kinds of new pressures and stresses. I had no idea how to deal with this. I was like a pressure cooker. Soon it began to effect my personality.

* * *

Diana and I celebrated the seat purchase with our first exotic vacation. Early that fall we took off for Tahiti and its neighboring island, Bora Bora. Surely I'd find solace and peace there. When we finally got to the hotel on the island, we'd traveled for twenty-seven hours straight. The hotel rooms were magnificent huts loaded with all the amenities. The huts sat over the crystal clear water of the South Pacific. There was a deck at the front of the room where you could sit and admire the spectacular view. I sat in the reclining chair with a beer in my hand, put my head back, closed my eyes and took a deep breath of the flowery smelling air. This was paradise. Then someone began sanding wood. It was very loud and very close.

I called the front desk and asked what the problem was. They informed me that the hotel was sanding and repainting all of the huts. I went ballistic. I raced to the front desk of the hotel and demanded to know why we hadn't been told prior to coming. I swore up and down, vowed to sue everyone and basically ruin everyone's life that was within ten feet of me. My ranting got me nowhere. Finally I realized that there was no escaping it, so I gave in and made the best of it.

When I got home I had other episodes of rage that seemingly came from out of the blue. I knew I had a problem and needed to do something about it. The inner turmoil was escalating, but I kept cramming the emotions down with the same old methods. My demons were lurking and I had no desire to face them.

***

Back at the CBOT errors were becoming my biggest expense. They were running at about twenty-five cents on the dollar. Most brokers' errors ran at about twelve to eighteen cents on the dollar, but for a first year broker, twenty-five cents was typical.

Nevertheless, by the beginning of November 1986 I'd managed to save $80,000. Not bad after the trip to Tahiti, my business expenses, and buying my seat and trading errors. That 80k vanished in November, in about one minute. It was November 6, 1986, an inactive Thursday, and Bob had taken a break. I would execute all the large orders our customers put in the pit.

I received an order to by 500 bonds at the market. As I was finishing up that order, the customer put in another order. This time it was to buy 1000 bonds at the market.

On a normal day, if there was a lot of activity in the pit, the big locals would be in the pit trading and I'd buy the bonds from them pretty quickly. It was so slow they weren't in the pit. So I had to buy everything I could get my hands on from many different traders. Instead of getting 100 or 200 bonds at a time, I got 25 from one, 47 from another, only 8, and then 50 bonds. Not good! Trying to keep track of all the bonds and be accurate in the count was a challenge. I managed to get my count correct, except I made a fatal mistake. I wrote a trade down twice.

I had a back-up system in place to catch these mistakes. That system was to hire a trade checker. The trade checker double-checked every single trade I made in the pit by taking the trading card the trade was on, and checking with the other traders' trade checkers. My trade checker missed the mistake. It wouldn't be caught until the next day.

The next day I came in feeling pretty good. I'd made about $4,000 in commissions the day before. It was about 6:45 AM. The market hadn't opened yet.

My trade checker was already on the floor checking through the computer printout of the previous day's trades to make sure that everything was OK. Suddenly he came running toward me waving the printout.

"There's a problem."

"What!" My heart leapt.

"Brian doesn't know the fifty lot." I grabbed the trading cards out of my clerk's hand and stared at them trying to decipher the problem. Right there on the top line of one of the trading cards was a fifty lot with Brian and on the bottom of the card yet another fifty lot. I knew I'd made a mistake that instant.

"Where are we going to open?" I asked my clerk.

He didn't answer me right away. Finally he winced and said softly, "A point and a half higher."

"Oh shit. What's causing the market to go so much higher?"

"General Motors announced they are laying off 29,000 workers and it's the biggest layoff in U.S. history."

"They couldn't wait one more day, could they?"

The previous day my customer bought a total of 1500 bonds at a specific price that I quoted. There was no going back. Bottom line, I owed him fifty bonds a point and a half lower than the market was about to open at.

I alerted Bob to the situation and told him to buy me the fifty bonds the best he could. He bought them on the opening, and my final loss was $83,000. That wiped me out. I had 80k in the bank and about 4k in my trading account. Barely enough to cover my losses.

Brian Porter was the guys name that I wrote down twice. He is one of the classiest traders in the bond pit. He's 6'7", very wealthy, and very funny. Jokes jumped from his mouth at exactly the right time, usually when tensions were high and I was *this* close to losing it. He was always calm and collected, even when he had hundreds of thousands of dollars at risk.

At about 10:00 AM Brian stepped out of the trading pit and came over to talk with me. I was sitting outside the pit on a bench. He felt extremely bad for me. He asked if I wanted to go out and party with him? Duh.

Bob said to go ahead and take off for the day, and he'd see me Monday. I think he was just happy I had enough money to cover my losses so that he wouldn't have to cover them.

Brian said to follow him to his house in Winnetka, a very upscale suburb north of Chicago. I'd driven my wife's corvette that day. It was a 1978 – maroon thing of beauty. I bought it for her on our wedding anniversary, and she appropriately had the license plate read: ANV GIFT.

We raced up the Eden's Expressway toward Brian's place and were there in no time. His seven-bedroom house was sprawled out on a huge lot in a beautiful neighborhood. We headed into his basement, which was a party animal's dream. Pool table, incredible sound system, full bar and numerous other toys. We started pounding drinks. By 4:00 pm, I was feeling no effects from losing all of my money. I was comfortably numb.

Brian was heading up to his house in Lake Geneva for the weekend, so it was time for me to head home.

Winnetka, IL might as well have been in Iowa in relation to where I lived in Oak Park, IL. There wasn't a good way to get from Brian's place to home.

I shouldn't have been driving in the first place. I had been knocking them back for six hours. What I remember about that drive home was that I did some extremely stupid things. In particular, that day I remember calling Brian from the car while I was still in Winnetka. I'd gotten myself lost. Brian started guiding me out of the ritzy neighborhoods to the expressway.

I came to some road construction. The street was blocked off for maybe a hundred feet. To get to the expressway, I needed to get down this street. I had no intention of turning around and told Brian that. He asked, "What are you going to do?"

"Drive on the sidewalk of course," I announced as I pulled up onto a manicured lawn. (You'll remember that I have a history of driving on lawns).

"No way!"

"I'm already doing it."

"Your out of your mind, Jim." Brian laughed.

He was right, of course. I drove the hundred feet or so on the sidewalk, causing minimal damage to the lawns, compared to my romp in 1977. (Probably because there was no one chasing me.)

When I got home, I decided that if I was going to continue drinking, I'd better get someone to drive me around, or I was going to kill someone or myself. It was Limos for me from then on. The rest of the weekend was a drug and alcohol filled blur.

Monday, I'd have to start over. I was so close to becoming a wealthy trader that I could taste it, but If I had another error, I'd be gone. I'd lose everything I'd worked for. The stakes were high. Bob could help to an extent, but if I continued to make mistakes, his confidence in me would erode. I was tense.

The flip side was I had a great deal of confidence in myself. I knew I could do this. Luckily, my biggest customer believed in my abilities.

Chapter 19

-Get a good job with more pay and your O.K.
   Pink Floyd

"Rage"

Early in 1987 my biggest customer was Morgan Stanley. Andy and Mark ran Morgan's trading desk. They were believers in my ability as a broker and were encouraging Bob to let me become a full-time broker. If this was to take place there would have to be a spot for me on the top step of the pit somewhere close to Bob. By moving to the front row, I could handle the smaller orders while Bob did the big orders. This was my ultimate quest but there was a problem. There was no room in the pit for me to stand next to Bob.

On our side of the pit, there were about seven brokers in the front row, and each of those brokers had at least two broker assistants standing on the top step in the back row. There were also nine locals on the top step in the front row and about three more locals and two more brokers in the back row. Altogether there were about thirty-five people on the top step on our side of the pit. This step we all shared couldn't have been more than 35 ft. across and 2½ ft. wide.

There just wasn't enough space, so in the excitement of the moment people pushed and shoved to be seen and heard. Everyone was jostling for position. Inevitably the pushing and shoving lead to people falling out of the pit, sometimes quite violently. The answer was to install railings.

The railings went from the top step down into the center of the pit. From above the pit looked like the pit had been cut like a pie.

In the front row, in our section of pie, we had Bob, Brian, Lance, Bill, Larry, Mark, Jimmy, another Larry and Alan. (Brian was 6'7" and Larry was 6'9".)

Nevertheless Morgan kept insisting that I create a spot for myself, so in about the summer of 1987, Bob called a meeting for the big traders in our section of the pit - the people who stood on the top step. We got together in Bob's office after the close of the market. He presented the new plan to the stunned crowd. This was how Bob went about everything, diplomatically, but pulling no punches. Exactly how my father would have done it. The results from the meeting? I stepped up to the front row in between Brian and Bill.

It was brutal. The market was now opening at 7:20 am, and I was drenched with sweat by 7:34 am. It was insane. I couldn't breath. But who cared how I felt? I was a full-time broker and I was in the front row! *I* should have cared about how I felt, but I stuffed the stress and emotions deep down inside myself and traded.

* * *

The broker is the middleman between office traders and the local traders. The broker must satisfy the office trader who is the client. The broker must also have a relationship with the people on the other side of the trade - the locals in pit. Being in the middle between these two factions created an enormous amount of tension.

The locals outnumbered brokers about ten to one. They were constantly in competition for trades from brokers. The most fascinating thing about this competition was how the locals would go about trying to get the brokers to trade with them. They'd berate them verbally. Yes, you read correctly. Strange way to do business. They told us that we sucked and could go fuck ourselves on a consistent basis. I'm not talking about every few days. I'm talking about fifty times a day, at the very least. The other brokers in the pit received the exact same treatment. I heard it when it was directed at me and I heard it directed at the other brokers.

This gets old quickly. Nothing took its toll on me psychologically more than this. I didn't know how to deal with it.

On the other side of the equation were the customers. My biggest customer, Morgan Stanley was fine, because the two people in charge at the desk, Mark and Andy. They knew what the brokers dealt with in the trading pit. They were excellent at their jobs and seemed to put a lot of trust in me.

My other customers were impossible to keep happy. They had little skill in dealing with the intimidating office traders on the other end of their phones. The office traders hated everyone in the pit, to begin with. They thought we were all a bunch of crooks. They demanded the phone clerks to confront the brokers, and so they did. On one side of me I was being told to go fuck myself, and on the other side of me someone was asking why I sucked so bad. "Why can't you get a better price on the order?" The office trader was never satisfied; hence, the phone clerk was never satisfied.

Furthermore, to score points with the office traders the phone clerks would scream and yell constantly at the broker assistants who worked for us. This put a great deal of stress on the assistants.

It was an endless barrage of verbal abuse.

The absolute winner in moronic behavior was Drexel, the now defunct trading firm. When I began working for Bob as a broker assistant, Drexel approached Bob to become their primary broker. From the word go, they were impossible to satisfy. It didn't matter what we did, they'd yell, scream or swear at us. If we got them good prices on their orders, they'd find something else to bitch about.

I took it all very personally. I wasn't able to filter it out. Their barbs hit me like daggers. They knew it too, and worst of all, they seemed to enjoy it.

The whole point is I was stuffing the emotions. My rage and anger would begin to build from the moment I started working for Bob. Looking back, I can see that I was doing exactly what my father had done, sacrificing emotions to make money.

I was determined to make money at any cost, because the money brought me attention and admiration. I sincerely believed that if I made more money my Dad would be very proud of me. He would shower me with attention and admiration. I was not willing to face the root cause of my rage and anger, because then I'd have to give up the money. I'd have to give up the quest for the Holy Grail, my Dad's love.

The suppressed rage and anger started to surface through explosive overreactions to things completely unrelated to CBOT. The first episode was in 1985. While bowling one night I got extremely upset because of my lousy performance. My reaction was out of proportion. It was only a game. Furthermore, it didn't help that I was drinking heavily.

I stormed off and marched over to the corner of the building where there was an exit door with a diamond-shaped glass window in it, at eye level. It had wire-meshing running through it for added protection. I didn't care. I slammed my right hand into it. The window gave way, but the meshing didn't, and it sliced into my hand like a knife through butter. Blood flew everywhere. I dropped my arm and another pint of blood dropped to the floor.

There was a bank of pay phones not far from where I stood. There was one person standing there talking on the phone, looking directly at me. "I've got to go," he said and hung up. "Are you ok?" He asked me.

"I'm glad I've had a few beers," I told him. "Because I can't feel a thing."

"I'll call an ambulance."

"Good idea."

Many people came to my aid while I waited for the ambulance. I basked in the attention but was feeling a lot of shame. What a scene I'd caused. Once the rage was released, shame usually set in. It was a pattern I wouldn't identify for years.

The ambulance took me to the hospital, and the medics stitched me up. I was out of the CBOT for two weeks. To this day, the long arcing scars on my hand are still visible, a reminder of the penalty for not dealing with my anger.

There were many other episodes. Some were on the expressway. On my way home from work I screamed at people who committed the smallest driving infraction. I'd chase people down, in my car, when they did things that had absolutely nothing to do with me. They'd cut someone else off, so I'd race up, cut in front of them and slam on my brakes. Brilliant.

Woe to the waiter or waitress who got my order wrong at breakfast. There'd be hell to pay. I went so far as to start bitching at the extra stuff they brought me. If I ordered two eggs and toast, and received two eggs, toast and potatoes, I'd raise hell. This behavior became a common theme in my life over the next five years.

Chapter 20

-Spinning, whirling
Still descending
Like a spiral sea,
Unending…
 Rush

"Filling the Black Hole"

In 1987, my career was soaring. The money was rolling in. There were huge checks every month: $10,000, $30,000, $55,000. I would gross $950,000 that year alone! My family now thought I was a huge financial success. My friends praised me. I was getting everything I had asked for. My life was going exactly as planned. What more had I ever wanted than this? Why wasn't I happy?

Looking back now I can see that interrelated emotional and psychological issues, seeded in my childhood, were not going to be ignored any longer. Something had to give. My physical health was the first manifestation of this. The mental and emotional stuff would follow.

A voice began to push me, ever so slightly.

"You are not healthy," it would say.

This voice did not taunt, did not abuse. It was just there. Quietly reminding me that I was not physically healthy.

I tried to get healthy - first a health club, then a diet; the usual. But my body revolted anyway. It was trying to tell me that I couldn't possibly continue the lifestyle I was living. It would say, "You cannot smoke, eat bad, drink, snort cocaine, take speed and live under the pressure you live under and then expect a work out to fix it. These things and good health cannot coexist."

"Bullshit!" I'd fight back.

Then, my body sent me a message.

I left the trading floor and walked into a little room off the members' bathroom. The room was a place where we could change our shoes and have them shined. Many of the traders wore special support shoes in the pit.

I flipped off my trading shoe and tried to catch it in my hand.

My back said, "Fuck you."
I couldn't stand up. I couldn't walk unassisted. Two friends had to help me get to my car. I'd be gone from the CBOT for two weeks, healing.

Two good things came out of this: first, my introduction into chiropractics. My first encounter with alternative medicine. Alternative medicine would change me for good, but not for quite some time. The other was that it helped me take the plunge into giving up nicotine. While sitting at home recuperating I found a service that could help me give up cigarettes for good, even after ten years of inhalation.

About a month after I returned from my back injury, I set out to the Michigan Avenue office I'd found to get that help. First I went to the bar across the street from the building and had one last smoke with a beer. I put it out, left the pack there and went to the office across the street.

When in the office, they assured me that it only took one treatment. They were correct. I never smoked another cigarette again. They injected a solution into my sinuses. To this day, I do not know what was in that solution. (What possibly could be worse than what I was already putting in my body.)? But I never craved nicotine after that. There was a big down side to this, though. I felt that quitting cigarettes gave me a license to drink more. Not exactly what I needed. Plus, I didn't feel like I had to try to get any healthier. I had the perfect excuses. I had already quit smoking, and I couldn't possibly work out because of my back. It was time to shut this nagging voice down and get back to work making money. It was time to fill that black hole.

* * *

Diana and I headed to Italy in March of 1987, for a vacation with my parents. It took fifteen hours to get to Venice, door to door. I didn't stop drinking the whole way. When we got off the boat in Venice to walk the few blocks to our hotel, I freaked. Call it culture shock or too much beer. It was a panic attack, and it was the first one I'd ever experience. It wouldn't be the last over the next two years. The cure for the attack was to rest for an hour in the hotel room and then go out drinking. I felt much better after twelve more drinks. The rest of the vacation was fun and a bit of a blur. I do remember getting sick the last few days of the trip, while we where in Rome. It was like I was in Mexico. (You get the idea.) It got so bad I had to call my doctor back in the states.

He asked how I was eating?
"Fine," I said.

He asked how much drinking I was doing.
"Fine," I said.
He said he'd take that as a sign that I was drinking too much. Back off he suggested.
I didn't.

Back in the states, I noticed that I was getting more and more restless, so I started filling up my time by doing things: going to bars, throwing parties that lasted twenty-four hours, flying to Vegas on a Saturday morning on a whim. Taking forty-foot limos out with ten people, destination anywhere.

One weekend, we had a guest stay over. We got up Saturday and had nothing to do, so I took $3,000 out of the bank. We headed to Vegas. This was about my sixth time there.

The parties we threw were unbelievable. I look back now and cannot comprehend how I did it. They got bigger and bigger. By 1987, they were huge. I'd buy the blow, and we'd have an instant party. We'd center the whole thing around blow. Let's get a limo, some beer, lots of coke, and we'd have a traveling party. Skip the limo, and we'd have a twenty-four hour free-for-all at our apartment.

Then, there were the Halloween parties that started in our apartment and grew to full blown events at hotels. The final one was at a nice hotel. We'd invited some two hundred people, had food catered and hired a great rock band and the greatest bagpipe band in the world. But, no cocaine for me that night. Just alcohol and mushrooms.

I was constantly trying to fill the hole or satisfy it. In mid-1987, we began designing our dream home. We'd build it with a great architect and have all the furniture custom made. We'd have to wait until 1988 to move in.

While I was waiting to move in, I got bored again, so I bought a Ferrari. It was magnificent. A black, 1979, 308 GTS, the last of the carbureted engines. I fell in love again between Lake Forest Sports Cars and my apartment. I became obsessed with this car. I couldn't get enough of it. We took the car to a small resort town, called Galena, Illinois; the first weekend we had it. On the way home, the five o'clock shadow hit us and cast a shadow off of the Ferrari and on the pavement that made it look like the 'Bat Mobile.' We applied for our license plates when we got home and received them in about two weeks. They read: BAT MBL.

The timing on these expenditures wasn't the best. Hiding around the corner was October 19, 1987, or 'Black Monday.'

Chapter 21

-He had a need to discover
A use for his newly-found wealth.
   Rush

"Dodging Bullets"

Black Monday will go down in history as the day the DOW lost 508 points. It was October 19th, 1987. When people take money out of stocks, which they did that day in droves, they have to put the money that's left over somewhere. That day, they'd flock to the bond market. I was in the pit that day and dodged the biggest bullet in my career.

The day started out like any other. We'd expected activity, because the DOW had been very volatile the previous week. When the DOW started to head lower in the morning, the bonds started moving up. By late morning the action was picking up. The Dow slid 200 lower on the day, which was big back then. Then, it slid quickly to 300 lower. The bonds did an about-face and went down like a rock to 'the limit.'

The bonds move in tics. 32 tics is a point, or a full point. The bonds tic like this: 85.00, 85.01, 85.02, 85.03, 85.04 all the way up until they tic 85.30, 85.31, then 86.00, 86.01, 86.02, etc.

The bond futures had a three point (96 tics) daily limit back then. Meaning that when they went up or down the limit, the market could go no lower or higher that day. It's basically a circuit breaker, telling everyone to relax.

I was in Bob's spot, while he was on break, when this happened. I got extremely busy, executing thousands of bonds. We went lower and hit the limit. Then, all this buying came into the pit. I had to buy 300, as we started moving higher. I bought them and completely forgot about them, because I was so busy. The stock market headed lower, and we skyrocketed higher. Bob came back from break realizing the market was getting busy. I stepped out of the pit to get my trades checked and make sure everything was okay. The market headed higher and higher, as the DOW plunged to down 450 points on the day.

My clerk came up to me and asked who I'd bought the 300 bonds from, because I hadn't written a name on the trading card. I looked at the card and the place where I was supposed to write down the name was blank, and I couldn't remember from whom I had bought it. I'd have to wait for the seller's trade checker to come to me to check the trade. However another hour passed, and no one came to check the trade. The bond market was two full points higher from where I'd bought the 300 bonds. That's 64 tics on a 300 lot. Or $600,000. I would be out 600k if I couldn't find the trade.

Time marched forward another hour, and still no seller could be found. I couldn't go asking around the pit if someone sold me 300 bonds two points lower. That might alert the seller that I didn't know who I did it with and he could decide to never check the trade with me. We were talking about 600k. People have done crazier things for less. The only course of action was to wait.

Three hours after the trade, someone came looking for the 300 bonds. It was a big local who stood just a few traders down from my left. I went to the bathroom and cried. The tension had built up so much over the last three hours I just couldn't hold back the tears. I was lucky that day. Many weren't. The bond market produced huge trading errors that day. A few brokers and locals lost everything. The S&P futures market at the Chicago Mercantile Exchange (CME) was worse. The stories started filtering over to us on Tuesday. A few were very successful, as I wrote early in the book, like Jeff. There was another guy who made two million dollars that day and retired the next. He circled the city block where the CME was located screaming from his car window. "Goodbye everybody!"

Then, there were the nightmares. Many people lost everything in the S&P pit. Huge miscommunications in the pit caused gigantic out-trades on relatively small orders, like ten and twenty lots. An order on which a broker would receive $2 per contract in commission, cost a career. (The S&P brokers made $2 per contract compared to the CBOT brokers who made $1.25. That's because the S&Ps are so risky that all the brokers refused to do it for less.)

Black Monday was a vivid reminder that nothing was guaranteed. It also told a story of the futures markets acting as the hero to a nation. Study after study conducted in the following years, proved that if not for the ability to hedge in the futures market, the DOW would have collapsed even further than the 508 points it did that day. They also concluded that the future markets were *the* difference between 1929 and 1987.

From that Monday forward, the Bond Futures market would change. One needs only to look at the volume over the next two years on the financial floor to verify that a major shift was underway.

In 1989, the volume in the bonds declined for the first time since inception in 1977. In fact, the volume would hold steady between 1987 and 1993, until reaching new highs of 99mm and 112mm, in 1994 and 1995, respectively.

The pit itself was also changing. With chaos comes order. The bonds were in chaos in the early 80s. Many people profited from that chaos. When people profit from anything in an economically driven society, others come running to cash in, too.

Many new faces were coming into the pit and into the brokerage houses' trading offices. Everyone wanted a piece of the pie. With new people came competition. Brokerage houses at the CBOT realized that they could lower the commissions they paid brokers with no consequences. So began a slow decline of per contract commissions paid from $1.25 in the early 80s to 85¢ by 1989. The brokerage houses started using two or three brokers as primary order fillers. This created intense competition, and a seemingly endless cycle of brokerage houses never being satisfied with the executions. They had the brokers by the balls, and they knew it. The complaining would only increase and so would the stressors that came with the endless complaints.

But I wasn't complaining? I would end 1987 making just under one million dollars.

Chapter 22

-I grow weary of the battle
And the storm I walk towards
When all around is madness
And there's no safe port in view
I long to turn my path homeward
To stop a while with you.
      Rush

"Changes"

Life moves relentlessly forward. Time stops for no one. Things change. Mistakes accumulate. Abuses do not go unnoticed. My cycle of destruction was about to come to an end, one way or another.

I believed that the bigger my bank account was, the better person I was. I thought that driving my Ferrari or cruising in a 40-ft limo made me someone. I believed these things to my core. To me, friendship was about hanging out, getting drunk, supplying the party with plenty of cocaine, and babbling on about nothing.

At the same time I was hearing a voice that nagged, "You're fat, ugly and doomed to be stupid the rest of my life." Then another voice would ask, "Why am I not happy? Why do I keep punishing myself?" Yet another voice would scream, "Fuck the money! Screw your CBOT membership – you're killing yourself!"

The inner voices were in conflict with my outer beliefs. I'd slip into unbearable sadness and depression. I couldn't stand the chatter in my head or the conflicting feelings – so I'd drink, or do drugs, or buy something, and continue in the cycle. Something had to snap.

* * *

In February, 1988 Diana and I headed to Calgary for the Winter Olympics. For the first time in the last ten years, I began to notice that my vacations were (like everything else) *focused around drinking.*

I was so unhealthy that I didn't have the energy to go to many of the events. I was tired, lethargic and heavier than ever. I found myself making excuses because the event was too far from the bar.

I noticed something else too.

We met one of the top plastic surgeons in the U.S. while at the games. He and his wife were extremely nice. The four of us decided to bug out of the games and head to Lake Louise in Banff. While there, I discovered another behavior pattern – using people for strokes. I'd spout my accomplishments, soak up the pats on the back, and move on to the next person. That's how I treated this couple and I wasn't happy with it.

Later they invited us to their farm in Kentucky, and I found that I had nothing to talk about. I'd already told them how wealthy I was and now I had nothing else to talk about. I didn't care about anything else that was going on in the world. I didn't read the newspapers or watch the news. It was bonds or booze.

I was beginning to question my beliefs, and another part of me was fighting it all the way.

* * *

Diana and I moved into our new home after we got back from the Olympics trip. It was our dream home, and we'd spent the last seven months designing our new, custom furniture and watching it come together.

I thought leaving the Oak Park apartment would help curb my drinking. Leaving that kind of atmosphere could only help. Well, at least that's what I thought.

My drinking just got worse.

I'd started drinking on the train ride from the CBOT back to Lombard, where our new house was. It became a ritual to buy two gin and tonics for the ride home. I met a new group of people - guys working at the exchange who rode the same train. They admired my success and were all seeking to replicate it. By the time I got to Lombard, I'd convinced my new friends to start partying with me, no matter what day it was. We all partied together many times over the summer months. I felt myself using them like I used the couple in Calgary.

Chapter 23

-All that you love
All that you hate
All that you distrust
All you save
All that you give
All that you deal
All that you buy
Beg, borrow or steal.

"The Black Hole Widens"

As I mentioned earlier in this book, I was unknowingly following a cycle my father started when he was my age, if in a more extreme way. His philosophy seemed to be "Never step on anyone or be unfair to anyone in business. You may, however, beat the crap out of yourself. <u>Sacrifice your health to achieve success in the business world</u>. This was perfectly acceptable."

I would follow these tenets, especially the part about beating the crap out of myself, right up to a fateful October morning in 1988. I was sitting inside my $400,000 home at my kitchen counter with a mirror full of cocaine, a bottle of Tangueray gin and a .38 caliber pistol.

***

I had achieved everything I set out to do since entering the Chicago Board of Trade in September of 1979. I had the admiration of my family, friends and co-workers. I was worth $2,000,000. I was on my way to making $1,000,000 in 1988. I had traveled the world from Austria to Tahiti. I had raced my Ferrari, bought

Rolexes, and traveled thousands of miles in limousines, thrown wild parties, built the house of my dreams. I was 26 years old. I had no desire to make it to my 27th birthday.

Money, trips, cars and possessions were not enough. The alcohol could no longer numb me. There was never enough cocaine. None of this could fulfill the black hole that resided in my soul. I had lived by the tenet "If I make money I will be loved" for ten years, but I was coming to the realization that to truly be loved I had to first look to myself. And so I did.

Despite my material success, my life was actually in shambles. My body was in an all-out revolt. I was grossly over weight, drinking daily. Hangovers were becoming unbearable. I was snorting Mount Everest piles of cocaine on the weekends and taking amphetamines during the day to give me the energy to trade. I feared getting arrested every time I left my cocaine dealer's house. I was having panic attacks. Though we danced around the issues, I knew that my marriage was in trouble.

The trading pit had become my hellhole. I loathed going into the pit because of the bitching and whining of the locals. I was overwhelmed by rage. I feared attacking someone physically - jumping on a local and beating him to within an inch of his life for all the abuse I'd received in the pit since 1984.

Nevertheless, the thought of confronting my problems was unbearable. My parents raised me to ignore sadness and to pull myself up by the bootstraps, so I was stuck in a viscous cycle. Yet at the same time something inside of me was waking up and sounding alarm bells. At first, those alarm bells were just conflicting and confusing thoughts and feelings, driving me to the brink of insanity. I couldn't see a way out, other than death.

* * *

Saturday, October 15, 1988. 7 AM.

I hadn't slept since Friday morning. I'd partied all night long, my friends had left and I was alone. Diana was gone for the weekend with friends. I slid into a deep depression.

As I looked at the mirror of cocaine and the gin and tonic sitting in front of me, I knew I had two choices. My eyes scanned the loaded .38 sitting on the counter. That was one choice. The other was to reach out for help and give up control, but that thought alone made me want to pick up the gun and pull the trigger. My mind raced between competing voices.

"Give up control? Ask for help? No way!" Screamed one.

"Death is not the answer!" waged another.

"But I'm so sad." cried yet another.

"How can you be sad? Look what you have! Your so lucky!"

"Fuck it!" Raged the killer.

"There must be another way."

I snorted a line and took a drink hoping to stop the mental chaos. It didn't work.

I picked up the gun and pointed it at my temple, then put it in my mouth. Tears streamed down my cheeks. I looked out the window through my blurred vision to see the trees swaying in the October winds. I slammed my eyes shut and slid my finger to the trigger.

"Pull the trigger, and it will all be over!"

"PULL IT!! PULL IT!!!"

And then suddenly, "Dad, where are you?"

I gasped and blew the barrel of the gun out of my mouth in one big gust. I let out a cry from deep inside my soul and more tears came. The .38 dangled at the end of a limp arm.

After a moment I laid the gun down, picked up the phone and dialed my friend, Dan Brennan to ask for help.

This call was the start – the first move to relinquish control – the first step to admitting I had a problem. This single step would lead me on the most incredible journey of my life. It would lead me into a world I had no idea even existed.

But first, I'd have to enter a new pit, the pit of my fears and demons.

End Part I

Part II

"The Second Pit"

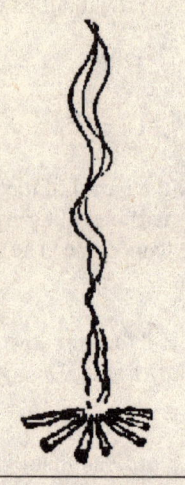

"God would never give me more than I couldn't handle. I just wish he didn't trust me so much."
-Mother Theresa

Chapter 24

"Shame"

*A*ttempting suicide is my call for help. It's the desperate act of someone who doesn't know any other way to reach out. Death is *the* common bond between all human beings. It's enough to get someone's attention. I didn't really want to die.

I called the only person who I knew cared for me for who I was, not *what* I was. That person was Dan Brennan. He is the only person other that my blood-family who has truly been there from the beginning. I have known him since I was 2-years-old. He could have cared less if I was a millionaire and a member of the CBOT. He could see through my bullshit in a second. I was Jim Goulding to him, period.

"I'm in bad shape Danny. Can you come out to my house?" I asked Dan that Saturday morning.

"I'll be right there," he replied, without hesitation.

And show up, he did.

It was a beautiful Saturday morning in October. Chicago usually had cold, rainy, Scotland-type-Octobers. Not today. The breeze was gentle and the sky sunny. Guilty sunny. The type of sun that ate at my gut and said, "You've been partying all night long. You'll miss out on me today, because you'll be sleeping it off. You should be ashamed of yourself!"

If there's one thing I can remember from those past days, it was the shame. This single emotion was my guide and parent for much of my life. It kept me in line, reigned me in, and told me when to talk and when to SHUT UP. It sat on mountains of anger, pushing the anger further and further down so it was indistinguishable from other emotions. Shame re-arranged my emotions like a brain surgeon. An evil brain surgeon. Working meticulously in the background day after day, silently re-wiring my internal circuits.

Danny came in. I needn't say much. He could read me. The items on the counter spoke volumes – the glass, the Gin, the cocaine spread on a mirror - and a gun.

He took the gun. I don't know what he did with it, but he took it. He put the Gin away. He dumped the powder down the drain. Dan had changed the atmosphere of my house by removing the three killers. Then he let me talk and he listened. This was my first therapy session. I yammered on and on about my feelings. Feelings that had been stuffed down deep inside my soul since I was a little boy. Feelings about my fears, anger and mistrust of people. Dan listened.

I talked about the realization that I didn't trust anyone. I went on about feeling like I'd been constantly screwed over by people in general, though I couldn't pin point who, or when, or even how. It was just a flood of feelings. I told of my misery at the CBOT and about the effort it took to stand in the trading pit day after day, listening to the verbal abuse. I talked about the stress of having employees at such a young age. Finally, Dan listened while I talked about Bob Laser. I told him that I tried hard to seek his approval. He was like a father to me. But he wasn't my father; he was my boss. So we are at the heart of matter. My Father.

Chapter 25

"Confusion"

A wise person once said to me, "Confusion is good; it's the beginning of movement." Unfortunately I hadn't met this person yet. So I thought I was in hell. Conflicting emotions were surging through my body and mind at the end of 1988 and early 1989.

Nevertheless, I would end up earning $1,000,000 in 1988. Not bad for someone who was in emotional turmoil. I'd never earn a million dollars in a single year again. From the end of 1988 forward a massive decline in my career would begin.

My marriage began to dissolve as Diana and I began to confront the "White Elephant". That's the elephant in the middle of the living room that we stepped around year after year, pretending that it wasn't there. The elephant consisted of emotional problems within our marriage that we continually ignored. Most people in this world have a white elephant in their homes. Without a doubt, confronting our problems was the hardest thing I ever had to do, except for owning up to my behavior, which was twice as hard.

* * *

We attract those people we need in our lives. At this particular time in my life, I'd been participating in a Wednesday night bowling league for a little over a year. There was a person in that league who held a *key* that I needed. She was a student of massage therapy (I'll call her Joan). Her massage teacher had given her and assignment. Joan was to give massages away for free, only asking the recipient for written feedback about the massage. Joan approached me in November of 1988 and asked if I wanted to receive a free massage from her.

I had never received a massage before and was quite un-willing at first. I was 5'10" tall and weighed in excess of 215 lbs. I thought of myself as fat and acne ridden. Which wasn't far from the truth. I had never purged my teenage acne. It was a never-ending curse. It was on my back, chest, neck and face. I had tried many cures. All for naught. The problem was, the cures I had tried worked on me from the outside in. It had never crossed my mind at the time that I should try to cure myself from the inside out.

I told Joan about my skin condition and my embarrassment showed. She said she didn't care and I was to come to here house the next night for a free massage.

Show up I did. This action was a "leap of faith". I'd take many in the coming years in my quest for health and some sort of inner-peace.

I arrived at Joan's house and perched myself on the table. When Joan laid her hands on me and started to apply pressure, something very close to a religious experience occurred. As she stroked my back, an inner voice awoke.

'There's another body in here Jim,' the inner voice said, as if to tell me I had layer after layer of protection on. Perhaps a suit of emotional armor?

"Oh my God," I said aloud.

She wanted to know what was going on, of course, so I shared the experience with her. When Joan finished with my massage I wrote my experience into here feedback sheet. Then I asked if I could come back again. She agreed. Thus started a series of sessions. What they did for me was nothing short of miraculous.

As Joan slowly applied the therapy to my body, something incredible began to happen. Raw, sad, deep emotions started to reveal themselves. Joan said it may be beneficial if I saw here teacher, who was versed extensively in dealing with exactly what was happening to me. Her teacher was a healer. I needed healing, badly.

In January of 1989 I had my first appointment with Joan's teacher, Karen Kobzan. When I walked into her office for the first time I found an atmosphere I was not familiar with. It was calming, candle lit and smelled of essential oils. Karen was a strong-willed woman, yet gentle and very concerned for one's well-being.

From the moment Karen began the first massage she encouraged me to let any emotions I was feeling to "Come Up". 'Ya, sure.' I thought. 'Whatever.'

This sort of thing was completely foreign to me. As she worked her way around my body, I found that I couldn't help but feel sad. That was a problem. As far as I was concerned, sadness was the pit of hell. Not only that, this feeling was taboo. Feeling, much less showing, certain emotions was not o.k. A tenet of my soul was, "Don't feel sad." So, as this feeling began to emerge I was sent into mass confusion.

I worked with Karen once a week, slowly bringing up emotions that had been trapped inside since I was a young boy. I needed more though. Feelings were revealing themselves by the dozens. It started to get chaotic. I couldn't organize my emotions. Hell, I didn't even *know* these emotions!

By the fourth appointment I asked Karen if she knew of any therapist's I could go see. She gave me a list of four she knew. I studied it when I got home, picked out a name on the list, and called it. Thankfully there was no return call right away. I was petrified and didn't want to bare my demons to anyone. Damned if I didn't get a call a week later. I set an appointment for March 21st, 1989 with Judith Palmer.

Chapter 26

"Leaping Into a New Pit"

The trading pits in the Chicago Board of Trade (CBOT) are a place of money. They are a place that brought me much notoriety amongst my family and friends. The CBOT represented a way for me to get attention. The attention was sacred to me. I craved it everyday, like a nicotine addict craves cigarettes. The more money I made the more attention I received. The more I received, the more I craved.

Yet, after many years in the trading pits, the attention just didn't cut it anymore. What then is there? Ah! Drugs and alcohol! Well, that behavior shot my body to hell. There was only one choice left. Leave one pit and enter another.

* * *

With great anxiety I went to Judith's office for my first therapy appointment. I'd been to a psychologist twice before in my life. Once when I was 15-years-old and again when I was 19. Those visits produced nothing. I wasn't ready. My focus wasn't healing. I had other ambitions - money and attention. This time would be different. I was ready.

Judith brought me into her office from the waiting area. Her office was small. Maybe 12 x 9. It had one couch, a big chair and a desk with a chair. One wall was completely made of glass. It looked out onto a busy street. Cars shot by in both directions. People were on the go, living there normal lives, and here I was living my abnormal life. I plopped on the couch.

My therapy began immediately tossed the ball right in the center of my court. She said, "How can I help you, Jim?" Her hands were folded on her lap. She was sitting in the big chair and had a stoic look on her face, utterly void of all emotion.

I looked at Judith and was at a complete loss for words. My anger took over, as it often did, and I began blasting this 5'2" woman.

"Aren't you supposed to know what the fuck I'm supposed to do?" I blurted out. "What the fuck do you *think* I'm doing here?" She didn't respond. I sighed, anger ebbing. "I don't know Judith. I'm lost and confused."

"Just start talking, Jim. Tell me what's going on in your life and why you think you ended up here, today." There was no emotion in her voice.

So I talked and talked and talked. Judith assessed and before I knew it, "Times up".

She instructed me to begin keeping a journal. I was to write down all of my feelings and thoughts in one place. I agreed and scheduled four more sessions with her, spanning a month. When I got back to my house I found a spiral notebook and began to write. Below is the first entry I made that day.

Journal entry 03/21/89.

> I just came from Judith's office. Anxiety, ANXIETY! Relax, let the feelings come up. I'm scared for Diana. I feel bad. I talked to other people about my problems.

> But that's what I do. I draw off of them and want their acceptance.
>
> I don't believe I'm actually confronting my mental thoughts. But somehow it feels natural. I'm afraid to cut myself off from the world and concentrate on myself. I'm scared to lose my friends and my support group. I'm drained! But it somehow feels good. Have I suffered enough? Something inside me says yes, and no.

The journal entry may not make sense. But that's the point. That's exactly where I was back then. I barely had a thought process. I was in severe emotional disarray. Inner voices were emerging and many of them were pissed off that I was seeking help. Judith would begin to separate those voices so I could identify exactly were they came from. Here's the next journal entry. It's a bit different than the first and you can see the denial begin to set in.

Journal entry 03/22/89, 5:20 pm.

> What a difference a day makes. I feel so much better than yesterday. But I am sad because our marriage is dissolving. But the healing has begun! I don't know about Diana though. She has a couple of tough therapy sessions to work through. I've got a pressure headache starting in the back of my neck. I use to never get

those unless I drank. Since I quit smoking I haven't had one. It's not bad though. Relief! Let the healing begin! I don't know what Diana and I are going to do. How are we going to separate? Who's going where? I'll talk with a divorce lawyer tomorrow. This feels so good to write. I feel strength inside. Daylight at the end of the tunnel. These hours are the hardest. The ones late at night. When I don't have anything to do. I don't want to drink. It's not natural or healthy.

I feel like I've climbed a mountain the last week. I know there's still another one to climb. I'm not scared. Moving out and separating does scare me. I wish Diana would consent to leave. I'm being selfish though. This is really hard on her too. Diana's friend came in today to comfort her. Her friend isn't mad at me. That makes me feel so good. Another of Di's friends called and she said she wasn't mad at me either. I can't believe the way people are reacting. They all say that this is not for them to judge. They just want to help and support us. Now that is just tremendous! I was worried, big time on how to deal with other people and friends on this issue. Bob Laser is being

> very supportive. Big help there. I really
> need his respect. Well, I'm feeling numb
> right now. Not much emotion. This, and
> I really mean everything about my
> situation, feels so normal. I am doing
> the right thing. This is what should be! I
> love and approve of myself.

I had only been in therapy for two days when I wrote that. As you can see I was in a very confused state. Feelings were bouncing around me like the metal ball in a pinball machine. They were chaotic and consistently inconsistent.

At the time of that writing my wife, Diana was also going through intensive therapy and we needed to get away from each other for a little while and try to figure out if we were going to stay married. If we separated, who would leave?

Without a scintilla of doubt, these first few days in therapy Sucked. Sucked with a capital 'S'. When I began to release emotions that had been stuffed inside since I was about 12-years-old, it was pure hell. So what in the Lord's name made me do it? Why, suddenly, did I decide to completely change my life? I'd made other attempts earlier in life to no avail. What made me think that I'd suddenly succeed? Good question after good question.

I've heard many theories. Some say there are psychological shifts at certain ages. One shift occurs at the age of twenty-seven. I was twenty-seven when I walked into therapy. They say that at these turning points we have a choice - to change or stay the same. I guess I chose to change.

You've read how the most important thing in my life was my career. From the moment I walked into therapy, and I sincerely mean the exact moment, my career took a 180-degree turn. It went straight downhill, like I was skiing the highest peak on earth. At the top was career glory, at the bottom, career death. Career death was the one of the single biggest fears I was facing in 1990. I was literally moving out of the Bond Pit and into a Pit of my fears and demons.

Why me? Not one of my sisters or brothers chose to face their fears and demons to this extent. The answer eludes me to this day. Part of me still believes that by taking the therapy road, I'm just indulging myself in my Irish pain. We Irishmen love disasters and pain. Always waiting for the next Stock Market crash or potato famine we are! Seriously, let me state that the process is agonizing and a constant reminder that I once had a couple of million dollars and a great career.

Journal entry 03/24/89 7:45 pm.

> I just couldn't write yesterday. I was drained. I talked with a divorce lawyer and that really sucked! So much anguish, pain and just feeling emotionally sick. I asked myself to turn off my brain, just for a little while. I told my brain nobody would know if I stopped thinking for 10 minutes. It didn't cooperate.
>
> Guilt is good for no one! But I sure am feeling allot of it lately. At this moment I feel really good about myself and I

need to hold onto that. I never thought it was possible to experience so much hurt and emotional pain. I asked for it though. It was time to deal with my emotions. Not to mention who I really am. What I am really about. I still get this satisfying feeling that this is running its course. That this was supposed to happen. I've been dealing with everything no matter how hard it's been. That tells me something positive. I'm looking in the mirror more and more. It's pretty funny how much you start to look better; I mean your overall appearance, once you start to approve of yourself. Self-love is the key.

Journal entry 03/26/89, 7:15pm.

I didn't meet with Judith Friday. I seemed to be OK. I knew it would be a tough weekend. And so it was. I could not see it happening any other way. I really felt good, Friday, not much pain. Saturday felt pretty good too. I worked-out hard. Tried to keep myself busy. I just sat in yesterday; I didn't want to go out partying. I didn't want to be in that atmosphere. Yet I stay home and drink three beers? And a bottle of wine? I feel like I'm in limbo. I've really been fighting with myself every time I drink. It's mostly by myself when I have to face up to my feelings. And after I come home from working out, I can't seem to shut it off. My mind will not shut up! So I seem to put my thoughts in a bottle on the weekend.

I can't stop thinking about Judith Coon either. Why would she want to help me? How can she help so many people at once? Why am I having such a problem with this? It's not her in general; it's the industry itself. Maybe I'm trying to deny help? I want Judith to love and accept me. I want to believe she listens to me and I want to believe she wants to see me cured. I had no other choice! This was all in the cards though. I knew I was opening up Pandora's box the minute I set foot in Judith's office. Judith's a pro and I have to understand that. People ask me how I handle my job day in and day out. I do it because it's what I do best. I think it goes the same for Judith. She needs to really know I want to heal. That I'm not trying to be selfish. I want to heal so I can live again. So I can help others. I keep feeling like I'm burdening other people. My friends that is. Today is Easter and it's the first holiday since this all came down. I felt like a charity case wherever I went. So finally I just came home sat down and started to drive myself crazy.

Why can't I shut it off? No one will know? I don't like myself right now. This weekend I went to Oak Park (The town I was born and raised in). I felt my roots. But that's nothing new. I've done that at least once a year for the last few years. My sister called and wants to talk with me. She wants me to hear her point of view. I'll meet with her. Today was a tough day. I really wanted to talk with someone. I'm having so many feelings. But I feel like I'm bothering people? Why don't I like myself? I've lost weight, quit smoking and have been working out almost every day? But I am still so hard on myself. Why?

When I became a broker I thought I would stop worrying about money. But no. I still put pressure on myself to make more and more money. Doesn't matter that I made a million dollars last year and this year. I must stop worrying about the past. Ease up on myself a bit. I can see daylight, if I'd just stop harping on myself. The

> problem seems to be that when I let up on
> myself it seems like I'm giving up?
> Losing my edge.

In that journal entry, there are hints that I was starting to have problems with my family. This just got worse over the next few years.

I began studying books on family structures and dynamics. (In particular, books written by John Bradshaw.) In my therapy sessions I began to talk more and more about what it was like to be the sixth child out of six. I talked about what it felt like to be on the receiving end of all the crap that went on in my family, day in and day out. All that crap rolled down hill and I was at the bottom of that hill. The more I talked the angrier I became. I began unraveling the dynamics of my family. I discovered that the way my family interacted was very dysfunctional.

During this period when I'd speak to my brother or sisters, they could hear the change in my words, tone and attitude. They could hear my anger and couldn't understand it. This created an enormous amount of tension between us.

On April 23, 1989, Diana moved out. We officially began our separation. She took up residence in an apartment a few miles from our home. I helped her move as did some of her close friends. It sucked. It was awkward, to say the least. We had been together for seven years and now - we weren't. It doesn't matter how much I'd tried to prepare for this event. When it happened, it was very difficult. Everything about my life changed that day. I was alone. Alone for the first time in my life.

Chapter 27

"Change"

Books. Judith and Karen were recommending them. It was time to start learning. Judith suggested "The Road Less Traveled", by Scott Peck. I devoured it. Karen recommended "BodyMind", by Ken Dychtwald, Ph.D. It became my bible.

I didn't realize it then, but my therapists were re-shaping my mind. They were changing my 'frame of reference'. We are the product of what we have experienced in our lives, including what we have learned from parents, other adults and peers. These collective experiences become our frame of reference. Since I was being encouraged to seek new experiences, new teachers and new peers, and because I was willing to do this, my frame of reference began to change. I began to change from the inside out.

I was lucky enough to have money, so I poured it into many different kinds of therapy. I was doing mental therapy, massage therapy, physical therapy and now I added a dietician to the formula. What happened to the outside of me was nothing less than stunning.

When I started seeing the dietician I ramped up my physical workouts. My body responded by losing fat and creating toned muscles. When I began in March of 1989 I may have weighed as much as 225 pounds. By August of 1989, just four months later, I was 160 lbs. It was a dramatic change in my appearance.

Would you like to receive some attention? Lose weight. People will notice. People will have all kinds of reactions. Although I would receive some great compliments, the reaction on the trading floor was anything but good.

While writing this chapter, I read an article from a daily writer in the Chicago Tribune. She had sworn off coffee. She said the hardest thing about giving it up was not the caffeine withdrawal; it was the reaction of her friends. They just couldn't believe she was doing it. Starbucks just wouldn't be the same without her! She went on to write that her friends hated her for it, because it was a mirror of their shortcomings. I could identify with her.

Everyone in the trading pit and every one of my customers noticed the physical change I was going through. How could they not? The problem was, I think I must have reminded them of their shortcomings. I was a mirror to what they were battling internally. I was eating well and exercising all the time. They weren't.

To be fair, I was also behaving differently on the floor. Where I was once jovial and funny (at least on the outside), now I was reflective. Furthermore, feelings I'd buried for so many years now started to surface. Anger, Fear and sadness refused to be subdued any longer.

Through the rest of the worlds eyes, everything was the same. But it was very different through mine. As I drank less, ate better and worked out more, my eyes began to open to a new reality. I was no longer willing to tolerate the moronic behavior I witnessed in the pit. I became angrier and angrier and I showed my unwillingness to tolerate it regularly. Trader's in the pit took notice and wondered what the problem was. Whether my actions were warranted or not, is not the point. The point is, I changed. Other's perceptions of me changed. I began to alienate people.

My relationships with my customers changed too. My perception was that I became more aware of them and more grateful for their business. Nevertheless, for some odd reason, the relationships began to deteriorate. My biggest client was Morgan Stanley. Mark and Andy ran the desk at Morgan and both were a key to my success, but by late 1990, they were both gone. New people were brought in and my relationships with them were strained from the beginning. By 1992 the relationship would completely fall apart.

Looking back on it now I can see that I was a very young man in a difficult situation. I was going through some rapid changes. These rapid changes just added stress to an environment that was already stressful. Maybe I was asking too much from myself? I was asking myself to completely re-wire my brain, change all my negative behaviors, like drinking and doing drugs, re-build my marriage and still keep a sense of professionalism inside the chaos of the CBOT. I was asking way too much of myself.

Chapter 28

"Group"

If there's a therapy that beats out all therapies, Group is it. In my experience, group therapy made the single biggest impact in my life. I believe that group is the most powerful and life altering therapy available. Furthermore, it's transferable.

Whether you're giving up cigarettes, suffering from the loss of a child or parent or need support because you're undergoing cancer treatment, there is nothing more powerful than the support of a group of people who are suffering as you are suffering.

I have been involved with, 5 AA groups, 3 therapy groups, 4 men's groups and 3 business owners groups. These groups had anywhere from 5 to 25 people involved in them. Some were intensive therapeutically and some were anything but intensive. I will write about these groups throughout this book (respecting confidentiality) and give you some insight through my eyes and my work with these groups, what it's like to be a part of something so powerful. Let's begin with the first group I entered in August 1989.

Judith was the center of my therapy. She was the guide. After working with her for six months she invited me to join a therapy group she and another therapist were running. It was held at the other therapist's house. Her name was Barbara. Barbara would become one of the most influential people in my life. If it wasn't for her, I couldn't have put this book together. As you will read in a later chapter, Barbara taught me how to think.

I entered Barbara's house on time and was asked to sit in the living room with the seven other people who made up the group. There was an opening on the couch and I took it. I said hi to everyone and Judith and Barbara entered to start. When a new person join's a group, they are introduced and the person gets to tell their story. After that, we went over the rules, the most important being confidentiality. "It's fine to talk about your work with people outside the group, but never, ever, talk about someone else's work and name them."

When I began to tell my story, I trembled. Sadness and fear consumed me. Several things stick in my mind about that night. One is the fear I felt when I told my story. I was very scared that someone was going to challenge me. Or someone would say something mean to me. I begged the group to, "Please take it easy with me." I was petrified. Thankfully, no one said anything negative. In fact they all had very positive and supportive things to say. They were all concerned about me and were glad that I'd reached out for help.

Say what? This was new. People were being nice to me even though I showed my emotions. No one laughed. No one told me to get my act together. They were genuinely concerned. This was a very different ballpark than the one I'd been playing in. This was my first experience dealing with a group of people that didn't seem to have an ulterior motive. I immediately became skeptical. What was it that they wanted? There must be something!

After my introduction it was time to let someone else talk. At least that's what I thought they'd do. To my surprise, the next person was going to "Work". That's the word they used. Then I heard, "Rage Reduction". Huh? What was that? I thought to myself.

This guy got onto the floor and laid on his back. Then four people situated themselves around him. I stared at them as they each secured an arm or leg and prepared to physically hold the man down. Then Judith knelt by his head. She asked the man what he was so angry about. Slowly he started talking about his anger.

Eventually the man began to yell. Then he was fully enraged. He screamed and spat four letter words. He struggled and looked like he wanted to get up and kill the person his rage was focused on, a person not present. The four others held the 'rager' down while the therapist encouraged him to continue. I freaked.

I sunk back into the couch and tears streamed down my cheek. I was hyperventilating. One of the group members who wasn't participating came over to sit by me. She asked if I was O.k. I told her that I could identify with the rage, and that it scared me to no end. I pictured myself on the floor doing the same thing, but they wouldn't be able to restrain me and I'd end up killing everyone in the room. She said, "I thought the same thing when I saw my first rage reduction. It's really nothing."

"You do not understand," I said. "I'll kill someone."

"No you won't. It just seems like that." She reassured.

I was trembling. The yelling suddenly stopped. I looked over and the person on the floor was all red in the face, panting heavily and starting to cry. I really wanted to leave - ten minutes ago.

Everyone situated themselves back on the couches. The man who did the rage reduction was "held". The point of getting held after a rage reduction was to replace the past experience's the person had. Some of us in the group were not allowed to show anger in the homes we grew up in. The consequence of showing anger was usually negative. Getting held by someone after doing a rage reduction replaced those negative experiences. Judith asked me if I was O.k. I told her I was scared. She asked why. I said I could relate to the rage and I'm very scared of 'losing it'. She was assured me that this was normal. Then she said, "Welcome to Group."

Chapter 29

"Marriage and the Ashes"

Diana and I had been separated for over 5 months by September 1989. We were both deep in individual therapy and both going through massive life changes. Divorce didn't seem to be in the plans, yet. We'd started marriage counseling with our respective individual therapists. All four of us would get together for marriage counseling sessions. Both therapists knew Diana and I very well. It made sense to hire them as our marriage counselors.

By all means the session sucked. I was in emotional chaos. Feelings were shooting out of me like a fireworks show. I hadn't the slightest idea what was going on. I put complete trust in the therapists, Judith and Barbara. Diana and I worked hard to resolve issues, find common ground and look for the love we'd lost.

We both discovered parts of ourselves that we didn't want to look at. Using Jungian therapy we identified these parts of ourselves. My parts were "The Bully" and "The Sad, Shameful Boy". The theory was that once I was able to identify when I was *in* the bully or the little boy, I could take charge and change my behavior.

Diana and I learned a fascinating thing. Our parts "Danced" together. She too had a bully type and a little girl type. When my bully took charge, it would trigger Diana to go into her hurt little girl. The same happened when she was in her bully; I'd go into my little boy.

And round and round we'd dance. Never getting anything solved. We weren't really communicating. We were just triggering the automatic responses of these uncontrolled 'parts'.

As the therapists put it, we were 'enmeshed'. Another truth became apparent. We learned that we both had married pieces of our parents and were determined to be loved by *them* this time around. When either of us didn't receive that love, we hated the other.

Of course, this was happening on an unconscious level. The idea was to become aware of what we were doing so that we could get beyond it, and take control of our lives and relationship. One of our goals was to replace the dysfunctional parts we found in ourselves with healthy parts. That process sounds straight forward enough, but it wasn't. It was incredibly difficult.

Lasting marriages are rare in today's society. Over 50% of marriage's fail. Theories abound about why this happens. There isn't a doubt in my mind that often the root cause is this unconscious seeking of a parent's love from a spouse. The idea is that as we search for a mate we are unconsciously seeking to repair a relationship with a parent. We're 'trying to get it right' this time around.

We first feel love on a deep, unconscious, and primitive level in response to our parent(s). This love develops in a healthy way, or an unhealthy way, or most often a little of each as we begin to mature. Then, as adolescence makes way for puberty, and our blood is infused with new chemicals, we begin to seek this basic love from outside our blood family.

This time around the process is less passive. We believe that we have control over shaping the love we seek. This unconscious process is complicated because, as we enter our teenage years, we have formed many of our own opinions from our personal experiences. Some of these opinions we are aware of, but others we are not aware of. In other words, it is all too easy to fall into a search for someone who will love us 'the correct way'. We wish to find in our mate that love we wish that our parent(s) had given us, or we wish to re-discover a love that we feel was present at one time, but is no longer available.

When we seek 'the correct love' from a mate it causes at least two problems. One is that our focus on the search for parental love does not allow an adult love between two people to evolve. In addition, the kind of parental behavior we seek in our mate may be dysfunctional – the result of a dysfunctional relationship with our parent(s), which may in turn be a result of our parent(s) dysfunctional relationship with their parent(s) – and on and on, down through the generations.

We are doomed to repeat this cycle over and over unless – unless we can become aware of what we are doing. Unfortunately the vast majority of the population doesn't realize the repetition of the pattern until they've been hurt, and hurt others, over and over again. When the pain becomes too great to bear, some may seek a therapist or a psychiatrist. Others will seek other, less healthy, ways out. Often this means the end of a marriage, or a series of failed marriages, violent behavior, and suicide.

Diana and I had founded our relationship on this unconscious seeking of parental love. I came to rely on

Diana in some very unhealthy ways. It was very uncomfortable to change this pattern and to begin to rely on myself and a new group of people for emotional support. I felt as though my insides were being ripped out from the depths of my soul.

In case I hadn't said it before, let me say it again. The whole thing sucked! The unwinding of the unhealthy tangled cords that Diana and I had built between us gave way about as easily as the cables that bind the Golden Gate bridge. To undo these cords took massive amounts of trust and energy, as we slowly un-wound them.

Diana and I continued to have marriage counseling, but our therapists truly believed (and were correct), that we needed to work on ourselves first, rather than the relationship. First we needed to be able to stand on our own two feet as adults. We needed to learn how to take responsibility for ourselves, instead of being quick to blame.

I would soon learn, in my first years of therapy, that going down to the bottom of our respective pits was the only way that we could heal. For me, it was the only way I could survive. To begin the journey we had to go down into the muck, to the bottom of the well, to the place were the ashes reside. We would have to dig into the fear and other unpleasant feelings that lay buried in the crap. From there, we could re-build ourselves. Following this we could forge a new relationship with each other as healthy adults.

It is my firm belief, after spending years *in the ashes*, that it's the only way to heal. To take the road down to the ashes is dangerous and is best guided by professionals and a community of others seeking the same. Otherwise the consequences can be disastrous.

* * *

Splitting with Diana was a lonely process. Add in the colossal changes I was making personally and depression soon set in. I became aware of the depression when I began to notice emotional responses to Karen's messages.

Karen worked a tad deeper than most massage therapists and I welcomed it. (Her massages could have been categorized as petrissage.) The emotional responses starting popping up in November of 1989. She would be massaging my calf, for instance, and my eyes would suddenly water up with tears. I'd become overwhelmed with sadness. I asked Karen what was going on. She said that it was her belief that people carried emotions within their muscles. She continued, if a person has been traumatized and has not released the event in some healthy way, then it gets stored in the body, particularly in the muscles.

"Okay," I thought. "Sure." But Karen's way of thinking increasingly became undeniable. Emotions were definitely welling up when she kneaded certain areas on my body.

The next time I went to see her, about a week after the first time this happened, I asked if we could do deeper work. I had read about deeper massage work and wanted to see if it could help me in any way. She agreed that it would bring me relief and agreed to work deeper with me. So we began what became a new way for me to release emotion.

Journal Entry 12-30-89.

> Deep massage therapy with Karen K. Working from lower back with her elbows. I cannot breath. Everything is stuck in my throat.

Karen and I worked deeper and deeper over the next month. Some of the work was agonizing. The emotions stuck in my body were overwhelming and frightening. Little did I know, this was just the beginning; Karen suggested I get "Rolfed".

"Get what?" I asked her. She told me that Rolfing is the deepest form of muscle tissue work you can have done. Then she said she knew a great Rolfer in northern Chicago and I should go see him. Fine, but what *is* it? What the heck is he going to do to me? She laughed and told me not to worry about it. She said I'd do fine. "Trust me." I *did* trust her and I took here advice. It was another leap of faith.

Splitting with Diana was also a leap of faith. This was a result of trusting our therapists' opinion that we had a better chance of reuniting our marriage if we physically separated for a while. I'd taken so many leaps of faith since I'd started therapy; I was getting use to it. My hope was, Diana and I would take a leap of faith together and get back together somewhere in the near future. We would.

By early winter of 1989 Diana and I decided to give it a go. Six-months after she moved out, she came back. We'd both taken our firsts trip down to the ashes and survived. Maybe there was something to therapy after all.

Chapter 30

"Letting Go"

While going over my journals from 1989, I noticed a common theme in my struggle – the idea of 'letting go'. There was the letting go of old thoughts and behaviors, especially drinking. Over and over I wrote of the loneliness of switching from one group of friends to another. The process was terrifying. But forward I pressed, because the old ways didn't work anymore.

As far as my career goes, 1990 was looking like another great year. The economy was about a year away from a recession. When the economy goes south, the Bonds get very busy. The result was that my business was picking up. I was busy enough to gross over $900,000 in 1989. This was particularly good because I was changing my spending habits. No longer spending frivolously trying to fill up the black hole in my soul with useless *things*. This resulted in saving lots of money. I was socking away tens of thousands. Between 1989 and 1990 I put away over $250,000.

Nevertheless business was subtlety changing in the CBOT and being a broker was also changing. The once volatile and super-lucrative Bond Futures market had become extremely competitive. No longer would the market move in huge swings like it did in the past and that meant less opportunity for everyone involved. This was especially true for a broker like myself, who executed orders in the pit for a commission.

The locals were struggling too. Unfortunately, the less money they made, the more they bitched and moaned. My customers became increasingly demanding. There was no satisfying them. In the past I could just drink away the verbal abuse coming from both sides, but now I was trying to drink less.

I just wanted to turn off my brain. Stop the constant barrage of thoughts and mixed emotions. I was trying my hardest to let go of my old patterns. Every hour of every day I fought my old behavioral patterns that craved alcohol. Let go and give in; became my new motto.

I was also letting go of the CBOT and the constant energy it sucked out of my lifeblood. So I'd practice, over and over, day in and day out, letting go of old behaviors and habits. Well, except for my driving habits.

One of the things I wanted to work on in therapy was driving. It made me nuts. At least that's what I thought. Soon I'd learn that driving, like anything, was exactly what *I* made it out to be.

* * *

"Get the FUCK out of my way, you stupid FUCKING PRICK COCK SUCKER!" came out of my mouth often, while driving. Why did people who wanted to drive 55, get in the fast lane? Who the FUCK did they think they were? They are nothing more than entitled Mother Fuckers, who wanted nothing more than to piss me off!

"It's called a blinker, you FUCKING IDIOT!"

"It's called a FUCKING GAS PEDAL ASSHOLE!"

"Your in the left hand turn lane, PULL UP SO WE CAN TURN TOO, ASSHOLE!"

And on and on. I couldn't drive a block without swearing. Frankly, it was exhausting, but I couldn't let go of the anger. I was so mad at society as a whole and people's complete incompetence. I became a *dry drunk*. Becoming a dry drunk is very common with alcoholics, when they begin to give up their crutch. Basically it involves letting go of drinking but becoming more and more cynical. I was drinking less and less, so I believed that I must be doing what I was supposed to be doing. Why wasn't everyone else? What was their problem?

* * *

I'm cruising along in my jet-black 1979 Ferrari, at about 6pm on the Eisenhower in Chicago. It was a few days before Christmas and I'd attended a party after the market closed. I'd been drinking (surprise) and was feeling no pain. The weather was unusually warm for a Chicago winter, the temperature hung at about 40 degrees. The sky dark and crisp. The ground was dry.

About 10 miles into my drive home I came upon a car doing about 55mph in the fast lane. How dare he! I flashed my lights at him to no avail. He slowed down. Now we were going 45mph. I suddenly swerved into the next lane, slammed the gearshift into 4th, and shot out ahead of him in about two seconds. Within another two seconds I was back in the fast lane in front of the offender. Do I really need to write what I did next? You know exactly what I did. Maybe you've done it too! I slammed on my brakes.

I'll never understand that move. What in God's name was I thinking? Just think about it. I'm really mad at that other driver so I think I'll get him to rear end my Ferrari? What's up with that?

Once, two years prior to this incident, I had been unexpectedly rear-ended in this car on another Chicago expressway. The cost to fix my car was $20,000! Now I cringe thinking what would have happened if this guy had hit me. It's positively the most moronic thing a driver can do to someone their pissed at. So naturally I did it.

I don't know how the guy didn't end up in my glove compartment after I hit my brakes. But he didn't and so I was off and running.

He caught me within a mile because traffic was so heavy, and he managed to move in front of me. Guess what he did? He slammed on his brakes. But he came to a compete stop. Not good. I hit him. Barely.

So off to the side of the road we'd go to talk it over. After coming face to face with each other, as the other cars whipped by, I realized he'd been drinking too. I immediately offered him $200 to get back in his car and get out of there, before a state trooper stopped and arrested us both. He snatched the cash and was gone in a flash.

Were all my driving incidents like this? No. I'd be broke if they were, but maybe if I'd had to pay $200 every time I behaved like a complete idiot on the road I'd have come to my senses sooner.

Fortunately, I began to learn it wasn't about them; it was about me. And I didn't like that one bit.

I asked my therapist, "How could this be about me, when they are the ones who can't drive?"

She'd put it like this:

"Have you ever tried slowing down and moving over to the slower lanes?"

"No"

"Have you ever tried practicing patience on the roadway?"

"Well, no, but they…"

"Have your fits of anger gotten you anywhere with the other drivers?"

"Well…I guess not."

"Then why not try to practice using some of the *tools* we are offering you?"

"Because people are assholes and they need to be told that!"

"I hear that you've been telling them this, and you said it didn't make the slightest bit of difference."
"Oh."

"Well?"

"Alright. I'll try."

Were there suggestions a miracle cure? Did I find paradise in the roads after these suggestions? No. Did it get better? Yes. How long did it take before I moved out of the fast lanes and slowed down? How long did it take me to be patient on the road? I'm still practicing. Am I better off now than I was in 1989? Completely. I haven't had a moving violation since 1997. That's five years. I haven't had an argument with another driver since 1996. It just doesn't happen any more. How? Practice, practice, practice.

Driving can be used as a metaphor for how much therapy has helped me. A person who drinks or is running around with pent up rage puts themselves in positions of harm. As I got control of my emotions and took back my health, I continually saw my driving become less and less an event. I have taken myself, my wife and my daughter out of harms way. Over the next few years I'd come to realize I had no control over the others' on the road. The best thing I could do was to slow down and move over. (Now if I could learn how to get those pricks of my tail that think I'm driving to slow!)

The whole point is I had to practice letting go of the idea of trying to control other human beings.

Chapter 31

"Affective Work"

"I hate you! You cocksucker motherfucker! Who the fuck do you think you are telling me what to do! I'm gonna fucking kill you!"

All this came out of my mouth again. Yet, I wasn't driving a car. I was doing *affective work* in group therapy. This particular night I had four people holding me down while I ranted and raved about someone who I perceived had harmed me in my life. Affective work can be done in many different ways and takes on many different forms. Rage Reductions, Anger Reductions, Two-chair, Three-chair and Re-birthing to name a few. Tonight I was doing a rage reduction.

All the emotions I had been burying since I was a boy were showing themselves. Before therapy these emotions came out in different ways. Seemingly uncontrollable ways. When I felt rage and anger or fear, they seeped out sideways. How? One way was blowing up like a volcano, maybe in the trading pit or maybe on the expressway, perhaps at my wife, Diana. I'd let it build up, then POW. Eruption.

Another way was passive aggressiveness. Example: I'm mad at my brother for whatever reason, but I'm scared to confront him. My sister calls me on the phone to plan a get-together. Harmless, but I find something in our conversation to pick on her about. This comes out of left field for her. She's blindsided and can't understand why I'm being a prick. But it's very satisfying to me, because I can get my anger out. This anger should have been directed at my brother.

Whether my anger about my brother was warranted or not, it didn't belong in the conversation with my sister. I believe passive aggressiveness is one of the most common things humans do to release anger.

Journal Entry 1/4/90.

> I began doing rage reductions on my father. I got some anger out. I can visualize myself doing it but when it comes to actually doing it, I experienced frustration. Frustration from not being able to get more out.

Yet another way I'd release my feelings sideways was to drink, then get in a fight or argument with someone who said something completely harmless (common in bars!).

It was easy to let go of anger in the trading pit. People verbally fight in the trading pit all the time. It is a normal thing to see, day in and day out. Of course, this was one of my favorite places to blow up. However, in group therapy I was learning a new way to release my anger through 'rage reductions'. This technique allowed me to release the rage quickly and productively!

I did many rage reductions from 1989 through 1992. Soon after they became 'anger reductions' because my rage had faded to mere anger. And then something emerged that surprised and horrified me.

Underneath the rage and anger was and immense amount of sadness. As I mentioned earlier, sadness was not accepted in the house I grew up in. If I experienced even the slightest amount of sadness, I might as well just shoot myself. It was an intolerable feeling. I would have done *anything* to not feel sad, but frequently, after a rage or anger reduction, sadness would come pouring out, and there was nothing I could do about it.

When this first took place early on in group therapy, I'd cry uncontrollably. It's the only way I new how to experience the sadness. Sadness simply represented mass depression to me. Now I needed to learn something different. I needed to re-program myself. My therapists and group members would help me do that. They taught me that these were *only* tears. It was *only* sadness. Sadness is only an emotion and emotions do not control us.

After rage reduction, on this particular night, I began to cry. Judith and Barbara told me to do something so simple yet un-thinkable to me. They had me pick a person I trusted in the group. I did and this person sat next to me and put her arms around me. What this did was re-program my brain and it helped me to begin building something new in my body; *A Safe Container*.

The container metaphor represents safety in this case. I was terrified of my rage and anger. I truly thought I'd kill someone if I released it. Now I began to believe that I could feel safe with my feelings. Where feeling sadness was almost unendurable before, and where anger seemed uncontrollable, group was teaching me that I could safely experience these feeling and get through everyday life, just fine.

I was learning new things. I was receiving new tools.
I'd take these tools and new experiences and run with
them. It was that, or go back to the old way. I'd already
tried the old ways and they didn't work. So I had
nothing to lose.

There was another astounding thing I started to learn in
group. Watching other's work in group was gratifying.
It helped form a common bond between all of us. We
were learning that we were not alone. Many of us
shared the same problems. Sure they weren't exactly
the same, but they were all about feelings and not
wanting to experience them. Hearing other peoples
problems in that kind of atmosphere is empowering.
We were sharing our deepest secrets and building a
tightly knit community. Every Thursday night, 3 times
a month, we'd meet, work, emote, support and grow.
The container was becoming stronger. The stronger the
container the easier it was to emote. And that's what
this was all about.

On these Thursday nights I might work for ten minutes
or forty-five Minutes. It depended on what was
churning inside. Some nights I didn't work at all. On
average, we all worked for twenty minutes.

Then Judith and Barbara began to offer the opportunity
to do longer work. They were holding a weekend group
called "Marathons". We'd meet Saturday through
Sunday. During these sessions each of us could work
for up to an hour and a half.

The marathons gave us the opportunity to go very deep
into emotional pain and stay in it for a long period of
time. Both Judith and Barbara would work with the
person who was emoting.

The group itself would usually set the tone for the day. One persons work seemed to trigger another's. So, if someone started out by doing a rage reduction, it usually was followed by several more.

Besides being another opportunity to purge unwanted feelings, or to work specific issues, Marathons were also about learning that we weren't alone.

Through my experiences, with many different groups over these last 13 years, it is now my belief that there is nothing stronger than community.

Chapter 32

"Rob and the Onion"

The first year in therapy was draining. I'd worked hard to get where I was and just wanted it to be over. I was tired from all of the changes I'd made and couldn't conceive that there were any more changes needed. Nevertheless, my therapists helped me to 'peel the onion', so to speak, and there was indeed more of the onion left – more fears and demons to face.

I walked into Judith's office and sat on the couch for another therapy session. The first question out of my mouth was, "How long do you think this is going to take?"

"For what?" She asked back

"For therapy to be over."

"Well, I don't know how to answer that. It's different for everyone."

"Fine, but what about me? How much longer do you think I'll be in therapy?"

"Jim, you'll know when it's time to leave."

"How?"

"You'll just know."

I was looking for Judith to set the parameters. If she would say I was fine, then I was fine. That statement speaks volumes because it means that I was looking for her approval. Like with so many people before her, I was still seeking validation from outside of myself. I wanted others to let me know whether I was OK or not. But I hadn't a clue that I was doing this. It just depressed me that she wouldn't say, "Jim, just one more year!"

In this therapy session, Judith said she thought I was ready for a different kind of therapy called 'Father work'.

"Father what?"

"I think it would benefit you to see a male therapist. I have someone in mind."
"Who?"

"His name is Rob Ahrens."

"You mean Rob the Rolfer?" I asked.

"Yes. He's a great guy who lives north of Chicago and I think you should call him and see if he can see you. How do you know him?"

"Karen Kobzan told me I should see him for Rolfing."

"Excellent."

"Well, maybe he can combine therapy and rolfing?"

"I'm sure he would if you asked him, Jim."

* * *

Rob lived in a northern suburb of Chicago called Evanston. It couldn't have been more remote! It took forever to drive there from my suburban home in Lombard. I wasn't thrilled about the hour drive there or the hour drive back. And that's *if* traffic flowed! If there was any type of accident (which was often), then my travel time skyrocketed. It was a difficult drive, but I never missed an appointment. That's because I found tremendous value in my sessions with Rob.

Don't misunderstand me. The sessions were brutal. Delving into my psyche was not easy and didn't get any easier with Rob. I was getting to root issues and they made me extremely uncomfortable. I kept going back to see Rob because I felt I had no other choice. What else was I going to do? Going back to drinking and doing drugs wasn't an option. So I kept practicing living with the discomfort of my emotions. This discomfort started to manifest as depression. A kind of depression I'd never experienced before. It was as if someone placed a black cloud in my soul, then wired a subliminal tape loop to my brain repeating over and over, "Death would be better than this."

My will to live was slipping away, while my therapists were uncovering layer after layer of the emotional traumas I'd experienced in my twenty-seven-years on earth. It was beginning to take its toll on me. For whatever reason, I stayed the course, trusting my councilors and new friends.

Rob and I also would start Rolfing sessions right away. We began to uncover a repeating pattern.

Throughout my life I'd sought out people who loved to step on me emotionally. They needed a victim, and I saw myself as a victim. From second grade to the Board of Trade, I'd seek out bullies like a drug to reinforce this frame of reference. Together we danced a dance. Never missing a step. The cycle fed upon itself like a snowball going down hill.

Rob would help me break this cycle through a process called 'Re-parenting'. It involved Rob acting the Father role and I the Son role.

Journal entry 01/20/90.

> Today I had my first Rolfing appointment with Rob. He is also my first male therapist. The session got a lot deeper than expected. Physically and emotionally. It was hard for me to trust Rob. I didn't really believe he'd be there for me emotionally since my father wasn't. Rob and I talked about it and that helped.
>
> In the Rolfing session he manipulated my right side first. My torso and diaphragm. At times I'd cock my head back and just howl with emotion as Rob dug his hands into me. Then I'd let my body go limp, loosen up and let him in deeper. We moved onto my right hip. As he dug in my muscle burned with an emotional fire. I yelled and screamed with pleasure because this was not painful. It was relieving.

> After the Rolfing was done Rob sat by me and put is hand on my heart. This hurt the most. He just placed his hand over my heart gently and my emotions erupted in sadness. I told Rob I didn't want to get close to him. I was scared. I told Rob I knew he wouldn't be there for me. I placed my hand on his and pushed it into my chest, cried out in pain and sorrow. Years of pain and sorrow. Then slowly I settled down. I told him we'd gotten through some tough layers. I was also aware at my desire to drink as soon as we were done.

I had peeled away a very frightening piece of the onion with Rob that day. Although I didn't know it then, it was one of the most powerful therapy sessions I'd ever had. That's because I was willing to let him in and tell him my truth - that I didn't trust him.

In therapy, some therapists have their patients draw up contracts. Not physical contracts like your lawyer would draw up, but a promise. A promise that was kept between the therapist and yourself. I had asked Judith in early January of 1990 to draw a drinking contract up. There was a small entry in my journal from the night after my first session with Rob, saying that I wanted to call Judith and have her release me from my drinking contract. I was dying to drink that night. New feelings were surging through me and I didn't like it.

The drinking and drugs I had been doing for the last fifteen years helped to build the onion. As I stuffed my emotions and refused to look at them, layer after layer of emotional turmoil was built. The only way to keep those emotions down was to numb myself. And numb myself I did. Now I had begun to reverse the process. Slowly pealing the onion. It was painful and unnerving.

Rob would play and important role in my recovery. Maybe the most important. For the first time in my life I was having a healthy relationship with a father figure.

Chapter 33

"The Opportunity"

Therapists offer us the extraordinary opportunity to explore and express feelings, even if those feeling are what you perceive as *bad* feelings, within the framework of a safe, honest, and clean relationship. With the proper guidance, we can discover and become aware of areas where we tend to get into relationship trouble, and then learn to respond in a more healthy way.

Journal entry 01/29/90.

> I'm in Evanston library. I've got two hours before I see Rob. My mind won't settle down. Emotions keep filling me up. I think I could cry at the drop of a pin. I hope I can release some of this at Rob's today. I can't put my finger on what these emotions are? I feel very dysfunctional. I don't want to be at work or play piano. Maybe I'm depressed? The want to drink is not nearly as bad as it was last week, after I saw Rob for the Rolfing session.
>
> Ever since I talked to Rob on the phone last night, (I called him because I was having so many feelings plus I needed

to make a therapy appointment with him), I've gone straight down hill. I feel angry with him. I felt it during our conversation. Where that came from I don't know? I don't think he understands the intensity of my feelings right now. He sounded insensitive on the phone. Very nonchalant. I asked him how long the therapy session would be and he said one-hour. I then asked him what was going on? Why did he sound the way he sounded? He said he was only leaving himself a half-hour for dinner!

I could really give a fuck about that! I have to kill three hours before our appointment up here in fucking Evanston. What the fuck does he want from me? It's hard enough for me to come all the way up here! This is difficult.

Journal entry, same day. 6:20 pm.

I feel a hell of allot better than I did three-hours ago. I talked to Rob. I described my anger to him. He seemed very receptive. I sat by him and he held me. I then talked about my frustration with communicating with my father.

> My anger towards my father. I cried a bit, but my body seemed to say, "Don't go to deep". So I didn't. I then asked Rob how I was supposed to function in day-to-day life with this new pain I was experiencing? He said I had to feel it. Actually marvel in it. Grow from it. Experience it and then, let it go.
>
> It felt good to sit by him. Have him be open and honest with me. I'm gonna take a wild guess here and say that Rob will be instrumental in my healing process. We've started a good relationship here. It will continue for a long time. At this particular moment, I feel solid. I need to hold on to that.

What was Rob doing with me in that therapy session and the phone call the night before? The answer is, he was being in an honest, clean relationship with me. Rob wasn't experiencing intense emotions like I was. He saw things much differently than I did, much clearer.

Rob had a problem with his scheduling. It frustrated him and he expressed it. It wasn't levied at me; it was just an expression of his feelings, a mere statement. I took it the wrong way. I thought that somehow, I was causing the problem. In the therapy session, Rob told me I had nothing to do with it. He asked, "Do you do this with other people? Do you tend to take on their problems?"

Bam! It was like he hit me over the head with a deadly realization.

"I *do* take on others' problems! Wow." I elated.

"What should I do now? How do I stop it?"

"Slow down, Jim," he said, chuckling. "We'll get to the solutions. First, think about the problem. How do you take on other peoples problems or how do you get yourself involved in others' problems?"

"O.k. I'll think about it."

By watching how Rob could experience frustration, express it, and find a way to deal with his scheduling problem without sinking into emotional turmoil, it helped teach me that I could also live day-to-day life without any need to be afraid of my feelings. Further, he was able to point out something that I didn't realize that I was doing. Once I became aware of it, I was on my way to correcting the problem.

By forcefully directing me through a relationship with him, he was showing me how I could have a healthy relationship with others.

I began to notice that Judith worked the same way Rob did. I was use to covering up problems and not facing them head on in a healthy non-threatening way. In the past, if I finally decided to confront a problem I usually went about it by yelling and screaming or just drinking it away. That's the only way I knew how. Now I was learning that there were other ways to deal with problems.

The opportunity my therapists and group afforded me went further than this. They were saying, "Come on! Bring it on! What are you feeling? Are you angry with me? Why? Tell me. I won't hurt you or verbally abuse you because your having feelings. I'll show you new ways to deal with situations."

My therapists and my fellow group members afforded me an opportunity to express these pent up emotions in a safe environment. Once expressed they all helped me to discover where the feelings really came from – a hurt from the past – or a time when I wasn't allowed to express hurt. In addition they were saying to me, "Project it on us and we'll help you sort out who it actually is that you're pissed at."

In therapy sessions with Rob, he welcomed the anger that I inappropriately directed at him. Then he guided me towards the real source of my anger. I was pissed at my Dad - pissed at the way he rarely communicated with me. I had to guess what my father was feeling and then figure out if it was directed at me. God forbid if I asked him. The reply was never kind or caring. It was laced with resentment for me being there. As if I was getting in the way of his drinking time. Or it seemed he was saying, "Haven't I done enough for you already? Christ, get your shit together! You're a never ending source of emotional problems!"

If it hadn't been for Rob, my other therapists, and my friends in group, I may have never realized that the anger and hurt I carried around, which caused me to blow up inappropriately at the wrong people, was actually stored response to the dysfunctional relationship with my father.

Chapter 34

"Practice, Practice, Practice"

Today is Monday, July 30, 2001. I just had a talk with my four-year-old daughter, Haley. We had a conversation about the secret to life. She stared at me in amazement when I asked her if she wanted to know the secret?

"Yes Daddy, yes!" She replied, wide-eyed.

"Practice, practice, practice." I said.

As I slide back in time, reading my journals from eleven years ago, I see the same tenet being spoken. Practicing was a common theme throughout my early therapy. Practicing being in my feelings without letting them control me.

***

In early 1990 to mid 1990 I was walking on new legs. Drinking was becoming less and less a factor in my life. I still hadn't given it up though. I still went back to the well and I was extremely hard on myself because of that behavior.

I eventually came to learn that being hard on myself was a pattern - one that I relished in. I was very comfortable in this behavior. I needed to lighten up. I went about addressing the problem slowly and carefully by talking about my feelings with my therapists and my group members - feelings I once thought to be taboo. The importance of voicing my feelings was and still is paramount in the process of healing.

I learned something else just as important as talking about my feelings. That was knowing *who* I should talk to about my feelings. Do not take that statement lightly. It is another key in the recovery process. (I will explain it further in chapter 45, titled, "Jung".)

When I faced talking about my feelings in 1990, it was like trying to climb a mountain of cliffs without tools. The mountain was practically impossible to climb. What I needed to do was go get the right tools. Everything I needed to climb the mountain was available. I just needed to be open to the possibility. I asked for the tools from my therapists and group members. I started by asking questions. How can I stay in my feelings instead of hiding from them? How do I survive feeling sad? Depressed? How do I go through day-to-day life and while experiencing such intense emotions? What will others think of me? How do I stop drinking? And on and on, I would ask, but then I listened.

I had to believe that the tools recommended to me would work. God knows people had screwed me a hundred times, why not again? Why should I trust that their so-called 'tools' would work for me? Faith. That's what it comes down to. That was my part of the deal. I had to trust.

The suggestions I received were honest and sincere. Some were off the mark and some on. I experimented with some suggestions and let others fall to the wayside. Some of the best suggestions I received I still use today. They are; working out, healthy eating, seeking alternative medicines, reading and practice, practice, practice!

I was also facing another mountain – inappropriate or unproductive behavior. Before therapy, the way I reacted to situations was anything but consistent. If I was pissed, I might say so, but often I said so in the wrong place and at the wrong time with the wrong intensity – over-reacting, in other words. Or perhaps I was angry and wouldn't say anything. That kind of behavior is just as harmful. It's like becoming a pressure cooker with all of these unresolved emotions building up inside. For instance there were times when I should have spoken up for myself, but fear blocked the way. So the emotions would stay inside and boil. I had no capacity for carrying those intense feelings around with me, so sooner or later I'd blow up about something trivial.

There was another thing too. I tended to react without thinking most of the time. I didn't take a moment to think things through – to count to ten, as they say. Instead, when I encountered uncomfortable situations that incited a good deal of emotion, I'd try to correct the situation right then and there – immediately – without thinking the problem through. Of course, it's not always appropriate or even possible to handle a problem immediately. In these situations we still need to carry on with our lives, until we can resolve the issue.

Instead of going on with my life, I'd get wrapped up in the problem. My whole life seemed to stop when I was experiencing this. It's as if there was no other part of my life except the problem and the resulting emotion. Everything narrowed down to a point, to what I was feeling then and there. For instance, say I was feeling ashamed because I acted out or lashed out at someone. Afterwards my whole life became one big feeling of ashamedness. How ashamed I was became the entire focus of my life. I would stay that way until I could numb myself or somehow resolve the issue. Another example, say someone had a problem with me, for whatever reason, I had to fix it then and there, or focus on feeling like a worthless human being until I could fix the problem. This was not a healthy pattern. It was a pattern that interfered with my productivity, my relationships, and my self esteem.

The key to breaking the pattern was, breathing and observing what was going on inside. Observing what feeling I was experiencing. Telling myself that I am not that feeling. The feeling does not control me nor does it define who I am. My actions define who I am. Ah ha! Say that again! 'My actions define who I am'. Wow.

Then, as an interim process, I practiced *not reacting*. I'd take the feeling that I was having and put it away until I could get to my therapist's office. Then the therapists and I would talk about the feeling and the situation. The beauty of this was the therapist could offer a non-emotional point of view. A view that wasn't clouded by intense feeling. It was an objective view from a third party. It was an observational point of view.

I think Judith said it best, while she was drawing an analogy of therapy to weightlifting.

"When it comes to your feelings, right now, you can manage to lift about two and a half pounds. We need to work you up to five pounds. Then ten and so on." How true that statement was. I couldn't bear how extreme my feelings were, and I felt I had no control over them. They'd bounce one way and then another, all over the place.

Living with my emotions and feelings, and letting go of alcohol, cocaine and speed, came down to practicing – practicing with my new tools – one minute, one day, one hour at a time. Slowly my behaviors would change.

I spent a lot of time addressing the emotions that emerged as I left my addictions behind. A big one was rage. Pure unadulterated rage. Where was it coming from? Where should it be focused? As it turned out, the family I grew up in was a central issue.

Chapter 35

"The Only Way Through It is Through It"

In late 1990 I was challenged to face suppressed feelings of anger associated with my parents and siblings, which resulted in sudden outbursts of uncontrolled rage. Fortunately my therapists were ready with exactly the right tools to help me through this difficult part of my development.

In the introduction of this book I mentioned that "The tricky part of owning your actions, behaviors and feelings is a conundrum." The conundrum is that one must sometimes start with blaming others in the learning process before finally 'getting' that we are responsible for our own experience, and that people only have power over us if we give it to them.

I was headed into this troubled territory – troubled even more so because of the dysfunctional voices of blame and guilt in my head that weren't really coming from me at all!.

Before therapy my rage and anger didn't have one. It was just there, popping out at the most inappropriate times. I needed to find out why I was so pissed off. That was a crucial and painful step. Finding a target for my pent-up anger was a huge success in my therapy, even if this was just a transitional device.

I would learn my rage was a direct result of ignoring my true feelings of disappointment and anger when I perceived I was wronged. Be it my brother, sisters, parents, peers or a schoolteacher; I didn't know how to speak up for myself when I knew someone was taking advantage of me.

Although I stated earlier that anger was an emotion widely accepted within my immediate family, my brother, sisters and myself didn't learn how to manage our anger. There was no guidance. The people we looked to, our parents, teachers and peers didn't know how to manage anger either. For me this resulted in a constant denial of my anger. Anything was better than rocking the boat. I learned it was better to keep my feelings to myself. This resulted in anger building on anger for years and years and years.

Anger is a difficult emotion to manage for anyone, but if a person doesn't receive non-dysfunctional guidance from someone in the early years of development it can really get out of control.

The sum of this equation was rage – uncontrollable rage. When I started to release some of the rage in group therapy I was extremely fearful of killing someone. I could picture myself going ballistic. I'd see myself harming anyone within ten feet of me - killing and maiming.

Of course, my therapist new exactly where they were taking me. They were guiding me to explore the rage so that I could learn what was behind it.

As I began my rage reduction exercises the first realization I had was that I couldn't rage about my family without there being repercussions. These repercussions were feelings of guilt and shame. Those two emotions had voices. The voices would present themselves like this:

"What am I doing? How could I say those things about my Father? I'm such and asshole!" Or, "I really don't have it that bad, do I? Look at what I have, money, a beautiful house and a great career! So many others have it so bad in this world. Why am I bitching at the people who helped me get there?"

These voices are described therapeutically as *Introjects*. We all have them. When we are at a cross road and a decision must be made, we go through a process of problem solving within our minds based on arguments and counterarguments, which can help us to reach that decision. Maybe we are deciding whether our child belongs in a catholic school or a public school. Perhaps we are deciding if we should have just one more drink. The voices of these arguments and counterarguments are the Introjects. They are the voices of reason, insanity, rage and many others. Some of us have calm, reasoning and supportive Introjects; some of us have unhealthy voices, like I did.

Introjects can be looked at as a hierarchy. You're at the top, then perhaps the next level includes your parents and siblings. The next level may be your teachers and peers. You'd keep building levels all the way down to the very small interactions you had with any person who may have influenced you, somehow. As a result, all of the people in that hierarchy will have something to say at one point or another during your decision-making process. If these voices are dysfunctional, and if you're not aware of the process, the result is a reduced ability to control decision-making and emotional responses.

The process of trying to become aware of, untangle and understand the influence of my voices was discouraging. I would become so overwhelmed I'd tell my therapists, "Fuck it! I can't go on! This is too complicated and it's sucking the energy out of me! I have no more strength."

Judith would say, "Just talk. Tell me what your feeling. No matter what the feelings are. No matter how much shame or guilt you're suffering because of those feelings, tell me about them. All of them." And then one day, after telling Judith that I just couldn't go on, she said something that has stuck with me to this day.

"The only way through it, is through it."

I didn't get it right away. It took years for it to sink in. Once it did, I was able to apply that strategy in many aspects of my life. As far as therapy goes, it was the single biggest piece of advice that has helped me get through the difficult times.

I forged on. Once I gave the feelings a voice, I was able to start to sort through them. I was eventually able to identify where they came from and why I had so many intense emotions about all of my feelings. Intense emotions that I do not experience any more.

For whatever reason, many of the people who influenced me during my early years were very dysfunctional. Once I became aware of what was going on inside of me, once I understood how Introjects work, I then had the choice to develop new, healthy voices based on reason.

Chapter 36

"Turning Point"

New Year's Eve had always been a time of getting together with friends, in a place where we didn't have to drive anywhere, so we could as we used to say, "Consume Mass Quantities" of alcohol and drugs.

This New Years Eve, December 31st, 1990, would be different. I'd been working with Judith, slowly trying to let go of my drinking. Twenty-one months earlier we'd put a drinking contract in place and I stuck to it. Judith let me write the contract on my own terms, such as limiting myself to only four drinks in one day and the exact days I could drink. I had whittled my drinking days down to three. Friday, Saturday and Sunday. This New Years Eve would be the last day I'd ever drink. And once I set the addiction aside, something wonderful would happen - something unbearable.

I didn't have any desire to tell anyone about my decision to stop drinking and taking drugs. This was the internal signal I was looking for, telling me it was time. In the past when I was going to try and give up an addiction, there was always a need to tell someone that I was doing it. I think I told them because I liked the attention and the pats in the back. But when I didn't have the desire to let anyone in on it, that's when I knew. This happened to me in 1986 when I gave up smoking cigarettes. I didn't tell anyone, until three months after I'd quit, and I haven't smoked a cigarette to this day.

I spent New Years Eve at home with Diana. We played board games and watched some TV. At 11:55 pm, I poured what was left of my gin and tonic down the kitchen sink.

It was over.

Years and years of alcohol and drug abuse, down the proverbial drain. I stared at the drain and asked for strength, I don't know from whom.

What was I to do with all my feelings that I had once drank, snorted and smoked away? The answer was to practice trying to tolerate my feelings and find ways to cope with them. Not an easy task in the beginning. This is where community comes in.

The therapist's I worked with were there if I needed them. Just a phone call away. However, they tried to teach us the power of *the group*. Or the power of community.

The group I joined in August, 1989 increasingly became a family to me. We all called on each other at all hours to get support and give support. Without that, I wouldn't have made it. It wasn't just about calling up a friend and bitching and whining. It was about giving too. I came to realize that I too had much to give others. I too was worth something. Being a part of our group re-enforced this over and over again.

The flip side was letting go of so much. Like my old drinking buddies. Like my old belief systems, my old hangouts, my old habits and finally, my belief that the CBOT was everything.

The CBOT was all I'd known, career wise. I had worked there full time since I was 17-years-old. Now I was about to turn 29. I had no college education and knew I'd never survive in the corporate world for long. What else could there be? I'd soon find out there was much more to life than the CBOT. Unfortunately, I found out the hard way.

Now it was time to live life without my addictions. Especially alcohol. To say the least, I was very scared. In the last 21-months I had learned that addictions are there for a reason. Most are there so we don't have to feel. The time had come for me to feel what was under the addictions. What I found were more layers of feelings. Hell, I'm still sorting through them.

CHAPTER 37

"Life without liquor"

Why do people attempt to give up drinking? Maybe it's an awareness of deteriorating health. Maybe it's repeated offenses behind the wheel of a car. Maybe it's ruined relationships.

Many people try and fail. Why? In a word, *fear* - fear of the emotions they will feel when the drug is gone. Fear of the unknown.

This chapter is about what the first year was like for me and the steps I took to keep myself off of liquor. The first part will include my actual journal entries from 1991. You'll see first hand what I was going through. The second part of this chapter will cover what it's like for me now, after ten-years of sobriety. The purpose of this format is to help ease your fears. If you're struggling to give up booze, and because of the fear have not succeeded, my hope is that by seeing that despite my fears and anxieties and backsliding, I made it through – and so can you. My hope is that you will find hope, and that you will take a tiny step forward towards reaching out for help.

* * *

Journal Entry, 01/20/91.

> My first writing of 1991. I have lots of things racing around my head this evening. So I've chosen to journal. I haven't had a drink this year. It's been

20 days so far. This evening, my Introjects were very prevalent. More than they have been any other time this month. I need to break this journal entry into parts. Good, bad and awareness's. Some of the good first.

My workouts have been fantastic. Especially my cardio. I can go longer and workout harder than ever before. I just plain feel better. I'm letting go of things. I don't second-guess myself as often as I used to. I am just dealing with who I am as a person. I don't rush around like I used to. I', going much slower. Time is not as intense as it used to be. My anger is more manageable. My feelings are more manageable. I'm letting go of money and power. My life is moving towards a different direction. Where I don't know?
Some bad stuff. When I'm trying to feel sad, or when I'm moving into sad feelings, my Introjects kick into high gear. 1. He tries to get me to do things. Tasks, chores, personal advancements etc. One after the other. It might me reading or home improvements or working on buying businesses. This all happens in about 20 seconds. Then it repeats itself. Until I work myself into a

state of un-comfortableness. Then my adrenaline kicks in. Then I can't sit still. Then I have to move around and do something. Sometimes I can calm myself down. But it's very hard. I think that this cycle is one of the primary reasons I drank. If I am to stay off of alcohol, I must learn how to bring myself down.

I've been getting headaches daily. Small ones, then I get tunnel vision. I'm experiencing tunnel vision at this moment.

Awareness's. I'm aware that life has its days. But it is easier without alcohol. There are much less ups and downs. Life flows like a stream. My little boy is much happier. I'm having fond memories from my past. Not just the bad memories, but good ones. My connection with my nieces and nephews has been great. I am seeing the world through their eyes. They are very simple and clear eyes. There is a bond growing.

I'm also aware that nothing is good enough for my Introjects. I mean absolutely nothing. I must discover where this comes from. No matter what I

do, be it play piano, work out etc.
Nothing is good enough for them. I build
it and it isn't high enough. Taming
these gremlins won't be easy.

TAMING THE GREMLIN:

Down boy.
Take a breath.
Enjoy this breath,
Not another,
That doesn't exist.
It is as it is,
You are as you are.
No more, No less.
Inhale, exhale.
No let it go.

Why so big?
Why so high?
Whom does it concern,
This thought you rush by?
Let go, enjoy,
Have fun little boy.

Do do do,
Rush rush rush,
Should Would Could,
Fuck Fuck Fuck!

> Days are as they are. They come and they go. I want to enjoy them in the here and now. This is the only time that exists. The present. It does not matter if you produce or do *things*. Relationships are the most important *thing* there is, other that taking care of myself. The people I interact with are so important to me. I care so much for people. What their names are. Who they are.

My job was to recognize that I had many different parts inside of me and to give those parts a voice. I was practicing expressing these different parts of myself. The good, the bad and awareness. Those parts had different points of view of the world.

The good and bad were value judgments, often inspired by an Introject. 'Awareness' represents 'living in the moment', that is, simply being aware of and appreciating life without value judgments. "Be here now" someone said.

This process, the process of becoming aware of what was going on inside of me, was key in staying off of booze. Why? Once we become aware of and then face our inner selves, we can then take control of our lives without the crutches.

You will also notice the poem in this entry. Where did that come from, you may ask? Suddenly, in 1991, I was beginning to learn that I had artistic talents that had been numbed away by alcohol and drugs. The poem was the first artistic thing I'd wrote since giving up drinking. It was the first sign that I had talents deep within myself. I began writing more poems. They just came to me. It was a wonderful process. I had no idea that I could write.

Another thing happened. I started playing piano. It was a life long dream. Once I set aside the addictions, my passion for many things began to emerge.

Nevertheless, there was more work to do. I saw it as 'I *must* play piano' and 'I *must* write'. Those messages were coming from a very negative place. I began to push myself harder and harder. This obsessed behavior extended to working out too. It's important that I relate this, because I had no idea that I was being obsessive. I hadn't discovered that this was a typical behavior pattern of mine. This is what I mean by having more work to do. Even though I was getting good results, I still needed to learn more about myself before I could gain greater control of my life.

Lets sum it up. There were two things happening in the first few months I gave up alcohol. First, my artistic side was showing itself and that's great. Second, I was pushing myself beyond my limits by obsessive behavior that I wasn't aware of. As I wrote before, 'The only way through it is through it'.

Journal Entry 02/09/91.

> I am in a depression. This really sucks. I can't think of a worse feeling. I am constantly trying to think of ways to move around this feeling. My Introject is kicking and screaming. All he wants to do is produce. But when I'm depressed, I don't want to do anything. I called

> Judith for help and she said it was ok to go stare at a tree if I wanted to. I hear that. But it's so hard to put into action. Sit and do nothing? Very very hard.
>
> My work is to continue to slow down. But it's so hard. I've also come to absolutely hate the CBOT. I spend all of my time thinking how I can get out. I hate that place. I would much rather spend my time helping people, in some aspect. Not work in a place that is just a cruel money making machine.
>
> I still haven't had a drink this year. It's truly wonderful. I never thought I'd be able to quit. But here I am six-weeks without a drop.
>
> Diana and I are getting along much better.
>
> My mind is not racing like it used to. But I'm aware that I worry about everything way too much. I also spend too much time worrying about what other people think about me. That's gotta stop!

Two things about that last entry. Judith said, it was ok to go stare at a tree if I wanted to. That's a simple

statement, but it took years for it to sink in. When it did, I went and took a long stare at a tree.

The other thing of note is that the CBOT wasn't fitting into my life anymore. It was beginning to dawn on me that if I was truly going to be happy I may have to give up a job that paid a million bucks a year.

Journal Entry 03/02/91.

> It has been much smoother sailing lately. Not easy, but more manageable. This evening I'm experiencing deep sadness. I'm needing to be depressed for now. Slow down.
>
> I still haven't had a drink this year. It was inconceivable a year ago that I'd be in this place now. I'm going to stick with it. I can't describe the euphoria I'm feeling right now. It's so wonderful not having alcohol hanging over my head anymore. It's taking a lot of practice living life one day at a time. Especially where relationships are concerned. I've done a lot of letting go around relationships also. I was too involved with everyone. I was making every relationship so intense. I'm not taking everything so personally anymore. I've learned to expect less from other people. Rob helped me with that. He helped me lower my expectations of people in

> general. If they have a problem with me, so be it. They will have to tell me.
> Life doesn't seem so intense and big anymore. Physically I'm down to 165lbs. My workouts are going very well.
>
> I started Rolfing sessions again with Rob. It is not as intense as it was a year ago. I feel more confident in myself.
>
> I'm aware that I'm feeling sad allot. I'm crying everywhere. I have to leave the trading pit sometimes and go in the bathroom so I can cry. It's popping up everywhere. In the car, at home, at work in the stores etc.
> I had no father to guide me emotionally. To play ball with me. To talk with me. It's like I was always getting in the way of his drinking or something. He just didn't seem to notice I was there. This saddens me deeply.
> I do not feel whole. There is something missing. Something keeps pulling at me. But what? It won't go away. I wish this voice would stop. Or show its face.

Euphoria. That's a word I used in that last entry. It's very common for alcoholics to feel this many times in their first year of sobriety.

Nevertheless, the hardest part of quitting alcohol abuse was allowing myself to feel depression without allowing it to go too far. I needed to experience it and deal with it to be healthy, but I knew that if I went too far the depressions would become intolerable and I'd have to drink to stop the feeling. This was another conundrum. I needed to deal with my sadness in a healthy way, but not allow myself to get emotionally out of control. That's why I drank in the first place. In order to deal with my sadness in a safe way, I had to constantly reach out for help, be it from my therapists or group members. Without them I'd never have made it through.

I was still pushing myself to extremes. A very telling sign from this journal entry is my weight. I was down to 165 lbs., from 215 lbs. And I wasn't finished.

I remember becoming obsessed with my weight and my workouts. I wanted my body to become perfect. I wanted my muscles to be 'cut'. Soon I'd reach 155 lbs. That's when Judith said something to me. She said I looked gaunt, underfed and wondered what was going on? I told her that I was trying to lose body fat. She then calmly confronted me. She thought that I was going to extremes.

I told here that I didn't have the faintest idea what she was talking about. She explained.

"Jim, there's no difference between weighing an unhealthy 215 lbs. and weighing an unhealthy 155 lbs. You're obsessing about working out and dieting."

I was dumbfounded and angry.

"Judith, I worked my ass off to get where I am! I have completely changed my life around, and your telling me I'm back to where I started? Bullshit!"

"I'm not saying you're back to where you started. I'm trying to get a point across. If I were to draw a line and in the middle of that line was calmness, and at each end of the line was extremes, we'd find you out at one end of the line or the other."

"Oh. Shit." I was plainly discouraged.
"This isn't about making you wrong, Jim." Judith began. "It's about recognizing your behaviors. You've come a long way. Now that you've gotten the alcohol and drugs out of the way, we can begin to look at you on a much deeper level."

This statement depressed me to no end. I was looking forward to *leaving* therapy. Not going to a *new* level. These thoughts sent me spiraling down the depression ladder. Judith immediately saw this and asked what I was feeling.

"Overwhelmed."
"Understandable."

Journal entry Sunday 03/05/91.

> I am in deep grief and sadness. This is very difficult. I must learn to slow down. I must get to these feelings. I'm so anxious. I've reached out to about seven people today. I asked for there love and support. I needed to know that I wouldn't explode. That I'm going to make it through this.

> I'm feeling tremendous anger towards my parents. If they would have just done their job! If Dad would have done anything!
>
> I can't cry! It goes against everything I was taught and I feel the need to let this sadness out. But I can't! My parents were crazy to have six kids. What were they thinking?
>
> I want my Dad to feel the pain I'm feeling right now. I want an apology from him!

In this journal entry, I was starting to feel more and more comfortable getting angry with my parents. I was really starting to blame them for everything that was wrong in my life.

I want to remind you of something here. I'm not advocating blaming everything on parents. Getting angry with my parents was part of a process I was going through. Remember the conundrum I wrote about earlier. To get to a place of peace, I first had to go through blaming others. So please don't throw the book against the wall! Read on. You'll gain a better understanding of the process as we go along.

Journal Entry 05/21/91.

> Diana and I are on vacation up in northern Wisconsin. Over that last few months I have been on an energy roller

coaster. One day I'm up, up, up. The next day, I'm down. I've experienced zero relief from my sadness and depression. I mean NONE! My anxiety is tremendous. Judith told me I've been carrying it around for years. Well, that's all fine and dandy. But how do I get rid of it?

Judith recommended I see a psychiatrist for anti-depressants. I wasn't very receptive to that. She wasn't very receptive to me NOT being receptive! We argued. In a way, I guess that's good that I had the courage to argue with her, because I'm very intimidated by her. Maybe this is progress?

I finally gave in and said I'd go to the psych. I'm too depressed to argue. I went and saw him a couple of days later. He diagnosed me as having a biological depression. He also said that I probably was obsessive compulsive as a teenager. He complimented me on all the work I've done trying to get healthy. He continued to tell me he wish he had more clients like me. That was cool. Whether he was being genuine or not, he won me over. So I am starting Prozac, a.s.a.p.

As I wrote, it was good for me to argue with Judith. That was a big step. I let myself become intimidated by her and that was a whole separate issue that we worked on for years. It was very healthy for me to argue with a person who was as mentally healthy as Judith. It taught me many things. The most important being, that I could argue with someone and keep it civil.

I certainly didn't want to take the medication. I felt as though she was just drugging me and putting me off in the corner. I expressed this to Judith and she replied that it wasn't her intention to do that. She wanted me to get some relief from the sadness. Then she said, "Many people see the world very differently from you, Jim. They see it without sadness and depression. I want you to see it that way too. I'm not saying you can't have your sadness or depression. I'm saying that you don't need to be in it all the time. The doctor said you were biologically depressed. This means it's no fault of your own. Many, many people live like that and never get help. Here you are asking for help! That's wonderful! I have no intention on trying to drug you. Try taking the anti-depressants and see if it helps. If they don't, then stop."

What stuck me the most was the idea that many people lived without the vale of depression over their eyes. That statement intrigued me. I wanted to live like that.

The next journal entry sums up how the anti-depressants worked over the following months.

Journal Entry 08/24/91.

Wow! I feel great! The anti-depressants have given me a whole new outlook on life. I'm not depressed anymore!

I've started a whole new form of therapy. 'Men's Work'. Rob has quietly pushed me towards connecting with other men. I went to Colorado with Rob and three other men on a retreat to Rob's house in the mountains. (Author's note: I have a separate journal on my experience in Colorado and will get to it in a later chapter.)

I wrote about it in my Colorado journal. In my other therapy work I'm certainly embroiled in it. I'm experiencing many different feelings. I'm extremely angry with Judith. I'm hanging stuff all over her. I'm putting my Mothers face on her. Judith trying to get me to look at my relationship with my Mom. How Freudian.

My Mom is the biggest bully I have ever met. She is the biggest bully I'll ever have to confront. I think I'm starting to move from an adaptive place to a confrontational place. When I get into

> confrontation with Judith, I'm very uncomfortable. I tend to move around certain feelings with her. Like the feeling of wanting to jump off the couch and choke her! Again, this feeling is miss-directed, but that's what therapy is. Miss-direction, then re-direction, then resolve.
>
> I've also come to learn about pumping myself up. I don't want to feel sad all of the time, because of what others' might think of me, so I ignore it and pump myself full of adrenaline to bury the sadness. My Mom taught this to me. It's exactly what she does.

My journaling may seem confusing. It may appear that I'm bouncing all over the place. I was. I wanted the entries to be unedited so that you can see exactly where I was, emotionally. Hang in there with me on the journal writing. You'll begin to see it become more and more concise. That's very important. The change was a direct reflection of my thinking process as I got better through therapy.

There are a few more journal entries left for 1991. If you take a look at the entries as a whole you can detect the clarity I was beginning to obtain – the clarity of the inner workings of my mind.

Journal Entry 10/19/91, 6 a.m.

The more I have my feelings, the better I feel. But it's hard work. I've spent this year without alcohol. That's allowed me to experience my grief and sadness. It's deep and consistent.

Yesterday in the trading pit, I started to get a pain in my calf. I tried stretching it and massaging it. Nothing alleviated it though. I called Donna, (my massage therapist), after work. I went to her place and we worked on my calf. The pain was so focused. From the instant she began kneading my calf, sadness leapt from deep within myself. It was as if she pushed a button. BOOM. I was crying like a baby. I got allot of relief from the session. But the pain came back a few hours later after I got home.

Diana agreed to work on my calf. She has been studying massage therapy and is quite good at it. She went to a seminar in Myrtle Beach and learned a new method called, "Myofacia Release".

Diana used this method on my calf and my leg. It's an unwinding therapy method. Hard to explain. But, it worked.

> She massaged my calf and then began cradling my leg as if it was separated from my body. My leg just began to shake as she 'unwound' it. After about 5-minutes of this I was a knew man. Pain was gone. Wow.

12/01/91

(Final Journal Entry 1991)

> Happy 30th birthday to me!
> I vowed to get my health back. I now have it. I have my life back. I have my marriage back. I have my self-confidence back. I have my feelings back. I have self-love back. I am walking hand in hand with my demons, fear, anger, sadness and a self-love that is still young. I used to do everything possible not to feel these emotions. Now they are my friends. When I respect these feelings, amazing things happen. I lose my desire to drink and do drugs. I become present in the here and now. The here and now is the only time I have control over. Not the past and certainly not the future.

The last journal entry was a huge leap for me. I was living in the present moment, (What a concept). I'd made it to my 30th birthday and was looking at life from a completely new set of eyes. But these eyes would change again. Then again. Then again. It was all a part of the process. Back on my 30th birthday I thought I was pretty much done with therapy. In truth, I had only begun.

* * *

In the second part of this chapter I want to give you a view from what it's like for me now, since I have over ten years of sobriety. I don't want to give away too much about what I went through between my 30th birthday and the present. Heck, that'd ruin the rest of the book. But let me try to give you some glimpses of the here and now.

As I write this, today is Monday, March 25, 2002. I'm not the same human being who wrote those journal entries in 1991. Not even close. Ten years of sobriety has brought much pain and much happiness. You might say, it has brought me exactly what life itself should be; some ups and some downs.

The difference between 1991 and 2001 is the size of the ups and downs. No longer do I experience emotions that soar to the top of Mount Everest then to the depths of the Pacific Ocean. No longer do I move from one extreme of the line to the other, as Judith's analogy stated.

I am living life without drugs and alcohol and I simply wouldn't have it any other way. As you will read in later chapters it has been anything but easy. Even now I struggle with many things. But I struggle less. Much, much less.

Remember; "Take it one day at a time."

Let's look at some of the other kinds of work that brought me to health.

CHAPTER 38

"Men"

I need to back up a little bit. During 1991 while I was in the midst of giving up liquor, I began a new part of my therapy. I had grown enough in therapy to start feeling comfortable to confront what was becoming my single biggest issue. Men as a whole. So I started 'Men's Group Work.'

"Why don't you all go fuck yourselves!"

I said that about three-thousand times in 1991. It was my general feeling towards men.

It would be easy to go off on many different subjects concerning men. My goal is to keep it simple. To accomplish that, I'll write about my experiences with Rob and the men he introduced me to. Most importantly, I'll write about the underlying issue, which was, "Searching for an emotional relationship with my Father". The only way I'd be able to have a relationship with my father was to confront exactly how I felt about him. The only way to do that was to continue therapy with Rob and get into men's groups.

I'd come to trust Rob more than I had come to trust any other man in my life. Not because Rob was nice, loving, caring or that he listened. I came to trust Rob because he let me be me. For the first time in my life I was able to completely open up to another man. I could talk about my hopes, fears, anger, sadness, dreams and views about the world. For instance, one therapy session in June of 1991 I told Rob that I really thought the world, in general, was an evil place and life basically sucked. Rob's reaction was unlike anything I'd experienced before. He said, "Say more about that, Jim."

I almost fell off my chair. He actually wanted to hear me talk about why I thought life sucked? I wasn't use to that kind of reply. I usually heard, "Get over it." or, "That's the most moronic thing I have ever heard." or, "Think about all the other people who have it worse than you do." or even, "God, you're an idiot."

Be it my brother, sisters, Dad, Mom, grandparent, peer, or schoolteacher, when someone important to my life said that I was an idiot, I believed them. Every time someone belittled my feelings when I spoke 'my truth', it was another notch in my psyche added to the "I am worthless" side of the scale. These statements helped shape and mold me when I was growing up. What they taught me was, "Don't talk about your feelings." And that is just plain wrong.

Now it was time to undo that mess and Rob was helping me do it by letting me have my say. So I ranted and raved about what a fucked up world this was and Rob listened. Occasionally he'd nod his head in agreement or he'd shift in his chair while listening. Then I saw him have a facial reaction and I stopped talking. When I stopped, Rob's reaction, and the ensuing conversation, is so important I'm going to ask you to pay special attention.

Rob looked at me and said, "What's wrong? Why did you stop?"

"You're having a reaction to what I'm saying. What's wrong Rob? Are you pissed at me?"

"For what?" Rob asked.

"I can see that you are angry."
"What gives you the idea that I'm angry, Jim."

"I saw your facial expression when I said that the world really sucks and I really do hate life."

"Let me see if I understand what you're saying, Jim." Rob calmly began. "You saw some muscles in my face move and you interpreted that as me being angry at you?"

"I guess so."

"Let me ask you a question, Jim. How did you feel when you saw my expression?"

"I was angry."

"Are you still angry?"

"I guess so."

"Jim, it's ok to be angry with me. Tell me that your angry and we can talk about it."

"I'm angry with you."

"Ok, thanks for telling me. What did I do to get you upset?"

"You made a face like, 'This guy is an idiot!'"
"Well, I'm sorry you thought that. Why don't you ask me what I was thinking?"

"Ok. What were you thinking?"

"Honestly, I don't know. But I can tell you I wasn't thinking you were an idiot. If I was thinking anything it was that you are brave for speaking your truth."

That's all I needed to hear. The sadness sprang from deep within. The tears flowed. I was sad for the little boy inside me that had never received this kind of nurturing from my Dad. And when I was finished crying, I got pissed. Really pissed at my father for never being there for me the way Rob was.

This therapy session with Rob was a massive turning point in my recovery. For the first time in my life I was able to talk to a father figure about what I truly felt inside. Most importantly, that father figure listened and responded with compassion. This was unlike anything I had known.

Up to this point my life experiences with men had been anything but pleasant. Going back in time I started to identify the men who'd hurt me again and again. Starting in grade school the pattern presented itself with uncanny continuity. Bully after bully showed up at my doorstep regardless of age. Some were grade school peers, some were teachers, and some I lived with.

I was looking for a father. An emotional relationship with a father-figure.

It began in second grade. The first bully I met, and befriended due to fear, was the first person I'd look to as a father figure. He was my peer, but age didn't matter. I can vividly remember this person and the power I gave him over me. I'd follow this person like a sick puppy dog from second grade through eighth, Constantly seeking his attention and approval.

He wasn't the only one. I'd do this with my grade school gym teacher and the vice-principal of the school. They were both outright bullies. The relationship with all of these people carried a common trait. We were acting out something that took two people. One had to be the bully and one had to be the victim. The bully received strength from this relationship by constantly wielding a sword of fear over the victim. The victim was solidifying the belief of worthlessness. Both the bully and the victim liked this place, as it became more and more comfortable over time. The relationship fed on itself.

Now Rob wanted me to meet other men who were having similar problems. Rob asked me to go on a retreat in Colorado with three other men and himself

"You've got to be kidding." I said with great apprehension.

"I'm serious. I own a cabin in the mountains just outside Denver. We'll go there for Four days and three nights."

"What are we going to do?"
"Trust me Jim. You'll be fine."

* * *

In July of 1991 I went to Rob's cabin with four other men, including Rob. It was on 130 acres in Jamestown Colorado, about 15 minutes west of Boulder. The 'cabin' was a beautiful house. On the outside, it was cedar and painted red rustic. The inside featured two bedrooms upstairs, a living room, dining room and kitchen on the first floor. There was also a deck that wrapped around the first floor with spectacular views of the Rockies.

We were here to do therapy for four-straight-days, but this was very different from the therapy I'd been doing for the last three years. This time there would only be men. That scared me. I convinced myself that if anyone gave me any crap on this retreat, I'd kill them right there. Funny thing was, I wasn't the only one thinking that.

We all were.

The tough guy image never got a chance to reveal itself. That first night, after dinner, we all gathered in the living room. I'd been feeling sad all day. Tonight that sadness erupted into tears and sorrow. It just came up. I was grieving loss – the loss of relationships - with my father, my brother and men in general. All of these previous relationships seemed to have been built on false foundations. They seemed to be made up of fear and anger. Both misplaced.

The other men gathered around and put a hand on me or sat close to me. This show of affection helped contain me. For the remainder of the retreat we talked, laughed, and cried. We formed close friendships that have continued through to this day.

There was an extra benefit to having these new relationships. Over the next few months something wonderful began to happen within my marriage. Diana and I became much closer and much more intimate.

This was a direct result of having healthy relationships with other males. As a male, I need healthy male relationships. Since I didn't have these in my life, I had been looking to my spouse to provide it. Well, she couldn't. Many men do not realize that they are doing this. It is a major frustration in many marriages. Each person in the marriage must have same sex friendships that are healthy, or they will look to their mate to provide it.

This is a very difficult concept for me to relate to you. I do not give the subject the credit it deserves. But it was another key in my recovery and probably the single biggest reason I'm still married to Diana today. I'm not going to pretend to be an expert on the subject. Just know that it is powerful and you'd benefit from doing research on it.

* * *

My previous relationships with men had formed around bars, a mirror full of cocaine, and sporting events, but there was something else too. As I met more men through Rob, it became quite apparent that we all shared a common bond. This bond was the lack of an emotional relationship with our fathers.

To realize that I wasn't alone in this was gratifying, and now I had the opportunity to explore healthy new male relationships in full awareness of this common thread. Great opportunity notwithstanding, it took a lot of practice to be with them in an environment that didn't include a table of empty beer bottles and a mirror full of cocaine. The result of my efforts was a new sense of peace that came from sharing with other men in a healthy way.

Chapter 39

"Career Death and Projection"

When I look back, I can see that the loss of my biggest client at the CBOT was both a curse and a blessing. But in early 1992, I saw it as a complete disaster.

Unfortunately, the career advice I was receiving from one of my therapist's, was not good. Heed this as a warning when you enter therapy, or if you are in therapy, let the therapist stick to what he or she does best; therapy. Seek career advice from a career professional. Let the career counselor know exactly where you are emotionally and let them know you're in therapy. The more truth you lay out, the better you'll be guided. Also, do not blindly follow the advise of a single career councilor. Seek as much professional advise as you can afford. Do some of your own research and then come to a conclusion.

I'm not bitter about my career falling apart. I don't know if I'd change the past if I could. It all happened the way it did and here I am. But if I can help you to avoid the mistakes I made, then great.

Slowly my goals and interests were changing. The fight and effort it took to stand in the pit every day was leaving me. I started taking long breaks. I'd go to the gym. I worked out for longer and longer periods at a time.

I was devastated when I lost my biggest client and then things only got worse. It was a snowball effect from that day on. In early 1992 I'd lose another big customer. Then another. Soon I'd have a minimal amount of business.

It was about this time that I decided to pursue a life long dream of becoming a Martial Artist. First I studied Tai-Chi. Then I'd move to a more intense form of Martial Arts at the Degerberg Academy in Northern Chicago. This would become my meditation. I became lost in the workouts. Soon I was working-out three straight hours. I practiced intensively - Kali, Jeet Jun Do, kick boxing, boxing, Jiu-Jitsu, Aikido, and grappling. I became consumed with achieving the sacred Black Belt.

I don't think I ever had a bad Martial Arts workout. It was such a natural fit for me. It calmed my 'type-A' personality. Plus, the effect it had on my body was incredible. I was becoming quite the physical specimen at 165lbs and 9% body fat.

I'd go on to study Bruce Lees' philosophy of "Jeet-Kun-Do" (No way is the way), the basic premise being, do not think that any specific teaching has the answers. Learn everything you can, and then draw your own conclusions. I worked the knowledge I gained into ever aspect of my life.

The biggest benefit to my studies in Martial Arts became the loss of fear. For years I walked the world in fear of other men and their physical power. For years I was afraid of a physical confrontation. For as long as I could remember I didn't feel like a man because I couldn't defend myself. That faded, very quickly as I became learned in the Martial Arts. And to this day, I fear no other man. I know I can defend myself or my family if danger arose. This was one of the biggest gifts I took from the Art.

* * *

I was facing a big problem. I needed to move out of trading at the CBOT and into a new career. Back then I viewed this as my biggest problem, not knowing that I had a bigger one. Luckily, I'd been saving money and was worth just under two-million-dollars. I could take my time trying to choose what I was going to do.

The bigger problem was letting the opinions of others overly influence my decision making process. What I know now, that I didn't know then, was that this was a repeating pattern in my life. I constantly let others make decisions for me. I thought that this behavior worked for me because it allowed me to keep from 'rocking the boat.' I thought that by doing what others wanted, I would be accepted and loved. In fact, I was giving my power away.

A hidden side affect of this stance in life is that it is easy to adopt or absorb the dysfunctional attitudes of the very people who we try to please. In other words, this stance of trying to please everyone, along with a lack of self confidence, creates a sitting duck for adopting even more destructive behaviors – and fears.

This happened to me back then. I adopted the fears and dysfunctional behaviors of others without even knowing it. Two behaviors I found in myself were projecting and blaming.

Projecting and blaming take on many forms. An example of projecting goes like this: I have a phobia, or a dislike or fear of a certain kind of unhealthy behavior (probably one I'm guilty of). A social situation occurs that could have any number of causes. What's true is that I don't know the cause of the situation. What's unhealthy is that I project my phobia or disliked behavior onto the person or people in the social situation. In other words, I become the accuser. I insist that that the other person or people in the situation are guilty of having my phobia, or are guilty of my unhealthy behavior. To put this in more concrete terms, if I know that I am capable of being disloyal, then I will suspect that others around me are also capable of this. I project my unhealthy behavior onto them. When something comes up that I don't understand, I accuse the other person in the situation as being disloyal, even though there is no evidence that this is true.

Blaming is easy enough to understand. I don't want to cop to my responsibility in an event, and so I insist that it is someone else's responsibility, hence the classic line, "It's not my fault!"

Back in 1991 I can remember what it was like to give up alcohol. When I embarked on that journey, I projected all kinds of things onto my therapists and group members. I was scared and it was easier to blame others than accept that I was an alcoholic. It was easier to blame my wife Diana for causing problems than it was to *own-up* to the problems *I* caused.

My therapists and group members signed on to let me blame them and project on them, and that's what I did. After just a few times of projecting my anger and fear onto one of them, I came to realize that it was misdirected.

As I write this, I am still in a therapy group, and I'm still learning about how to deal with projecting and blaming. These things can sneak up on you. We really have to be aware and 'in the moment' to catch ourselves at it before we end up with a foot in our mouth.

For instance, there is a member in that group who was talking and I felt myself getting really pissed off and angry. I stopped and asked myself, why? What is it that's irking me? What I found when I looked inside myself was fear. This person had pushed a fear button in me. That fear was linked to my want for attention from others, the want to be noticed and acknowledged as a distinct and special human being. This is a basic human concern. My fear was that this person would take this away from me, or somehow diminish me in the eyes of the rest of the group. Another similar example would be fear that someone else would hog the limelight. This would directly interfere with me being the center of attention. And that would make me angry.

What's true, of course, is that our focus should be on learning how to make ourselves into the best person we can be, instead of being needy about attention. The attention of others will be a natural, reciprocal part of being a good listener, being compassionate, being considerate, being interesting because we bring our interests and knowledge to the group, etc.; in other words, having good social skills. When we practice good social skills, there is always plenty of limelight to go around. There is no need to fear otherwise. And when we are needy about attention, we shoot ourselves in the foot, because it's the best way to chase people away.

Another example; My daughter wants me to play with her. Well, I have a lot of trouble with unstructured play. I dislike it. But that's the way a four-year-old plays. When she asks me to play and I find myself getting irritated or angry with her, I must stop and ask myself where the feelings are coming from. The last thing I want to do is project the problem onto her. That's the way dysfunctional behavior gets passed on from generation to generation.

Often, when I've found myself becoming angry with one of my siblings, I've found that the real source of the anger has little or nothing to do with what they are saying at the moment. Instead they are inadvertently pushing triggers hooked to anger that I still carry as a result of my reactions as a child to how I was treated when I was growing up.

Do you project and blame? Ask yourself when you begin to become angry with someone. Are you reacting to what is being said in the moment, or is this person simply inadvertently hooking into anger that you're carrying around from long ago? Maybe what they are doing is something that you don't like in yourself – this happens. If you find yourself over-reacting to situations, you've probably got work to do. In other words, if you react in a much bigger way than what is appropriate for the situation, there's probably something else going on that needs to be dealt with.

* * *

I had been in therapy for four years by 1993. I had quit drinking, doing drugs, and my marriage was back together. I had made a lot of progress, but I still felt like a psychological mess.

Not only that, my career was coming to and end at the CBOT. There were many options within the CBOT, but I was so burned out. I really wanted to leave in

1993 and should of. Instead, I stuck it out. I was trying not to make an irrational decision. I was trying my best to heed the advice of all my councilors and take into consideration their opinions and those of friends. But that's hindsight for you. What I did at the time is what I was capable of doing. No sense in beating myself up now because I have a broader perspective – or anyone else! Instead, we move on, hopefully, more enlightened than before.

Chapter 40

"Cutting the Cord"

*Y*ou cannot divorce your family. If you're a minor you can legally divorce yourself from your family, but that's not what I'm talking about.

I'm talking emotionally, psychologically and genetically. You can tell your siblings and parents to fuck off, that you never want to speak to them again, and you can move to the other side of the globe. It doesn't matter, because they're inside of you.

Nevertheless, what I needed to do in 1992 was to cut the cord - get a separation. Separating from my family would be the major focus, of my therapy, for the next two years.

In late 1991, just before Christmas, I started calling my various family members to tell them that I wasn't coming to the Christmas festivities. I also told them that I didn't want any of them to contact me until I contacted them. What ensued was all out mass chaos. They were pissed.

* * *

What exactly was it that happened while I was growing up? What did my family do to me during my youth that would make me hate them so much? Was I physically beat? Locked in the basement with no food? What was it they did?

I don't know. I was never hit, never locked in the basement or a closet or anywhere else for that matter. It has been very difficult to pin down exactly what went on while I was growing up, that resulted in my destructive behaviors.

My therapists and I mulled this over year in and year out. I can't say we came up with a name for it. I wish that I could put a name on it, like a disease. This would have made my journey that much easier. My therapists could have prescribed a specific course of action for me, but that's not the way it went.

One of my sisters told me that she was very sure a family friend had sexually molested me when I was young. When I heard this, though I couldn't remember any incident, I thought that maybe the disease had been found. I investigated it to the best of my abilities and really couldn't come up with any evidence to support it. Maybe I was. Maybe I wasn't.

Theories came and went. Maybe my mother ignored me when I cried as a baby. After all I was the sixth child and the oldest was eight when I was born. That's a lot of kids! Research has been done on 'ignored babies'. Those babies usually grow up to be like me. This seemed promising. But my mother insists that it's just not true. Who should I believe?

In my research, I discovered that I was not alone. There are millions like me – people who cannot put a name to the cause of their destructive behaviors. This was the most difficult thing to deal with while I was recovering. The answer is that 'it' was probably not just one thing. More likely it was a tangled complex of reasons.

The closest I can come to putting a name to it is 'psychological abuse', but there was no malicious intent involved.

By now you must suspect that the relationships in my family, like so many others, were simply dysfunctional. You'd be exactly right. As a result of destructive attitudes, problems with communication, emotional remoteness and unhealthy responses to everyday stress, I grew up with subtle, yet powerful, misperceptions about myself and the world around me. These misperceptions colored my relationships outside of the family as well.

When I finally gave up drugs and alcohol and my brain cleared, the effects of growing up in a dysfunctional environment, and participating in dysfunctional relationships outside of the family, became painfully clear. When the unhealthy habits, perceptions and behaviors became more clear, my therapists and I had something to work with – a place to start.

What we found was a long, convoluted path through thorny issues that I had been unknowingly carrying around for most of my life. There was no simple way, no simple method, no simple answer. Instead, as I said before, the only way through it – was through it – so that we could mend what we found along the way.

For instance, there were voices (not literal voices, but distinct voice-like thoughts that come racing through our heads sometimes) that screamed things like, "Look at what you have compared to others in this world. Look at what you had as a kid - a roof over your head, food on the table, clothes on your back and good schools. So what are you complaining about?" or, "The sacrifices that were made so you could live like that were enormous. Jeesh, your grandfather came over on the boat in 1916 with about $50 in his pocket! Your great grandfather did the same thing in the late 1800's! What the F*** is your problem?" I heard statements like these over and over.

The problem is that these words are judgmental and offer no discourse whatsoever. There is no compassion in these words – no attempt at understanding. They represent an end to communication – not a beginning. In fact these statements are bullying. In my therapy I discovered that the problem with listening to these words is that they were very destructive to my self esteem.

One effect of this judgmental barrage was to go into a psychic self-defense mode. I shut down my feelings. I was shutting down the feelings that were screaming, "I am so sad. I am so mad!", but it didn't matter how many times I pulled myself up by my bootstraps and tried to ignore them. They remained, and so I did what I had to do to shut them up – hence my self-destructive behaviors.

This cannot be denied. When I decided to ignore those negative statements, when I gave myself permission to begin stating exactly how I felt, when I began to learn how to deal with my emotions, when I began to see myself and the world in a different light, a miraculous thing began to happen. There was no longer any need for my self-destructive behaviors.

As I was studying "Generations" by Strauss and Howe, I was stunned at the way generations react to each other. I'm not going to go into a detailed study of the book here. The book is too important for me to try and capsulate it here. Read it. You will not be disappointed.

I was impressed by the evidence set forth by the authors.

I will say this. The last wave of the Baby Boomers and the first wave of Gen-X'ers got the short end of the stick. We were discarded as 'irrelevant' and 'under motivated' by society. Nobody cared about our point of view. We were shoved aside and told to do it on our own. After reading Generations, I was so relieved. I identified so heavily with the Gen-X'ers. At least this part wasn't just me.

There's no blame here. Instead, finding the reasons for my troubled psyche gave me hope and renewed strength. What a relief to discover some evidence that I'm not simply and hopelessly loony.

During this period of time my self-destructive behaviors started vanishing. No booze, no drugs, no overeating. Furthermore, after years of this, I was able to come to a place of complete thankfulness for many things. I was able to come into a state of grace.

I will cover this in a few chapters because we are almost at the end of the road.

* * *

Earlier I wrote about the author, John Bradshaw. His work on families is enlightening, educational and right on the money. I can't say enough about how much his books helped me through the biggest challenge I was facing in late 1991 and early 1992. I of course also highly recommend "Generations" by Strauss and Howe.

Chapter 41

"Staying the Course"

My family went ballistic regarding my decision to distance myself from them. The news that I wasn't coming to Christmas and further that I'd asked people not to contact me had ripped through the family faster than the speed of light. The family acted as a single unit. Except for one of my sisters who'd been going to therapy and she told me, "I completely understand why you are doing this."

Bradshaw was right. He states in many of his books that the family will move as a unit. Family members will look to the decision maker to see how *she or he* will react personally, and then follow suit. The decision maker was my Mother and she was sad. That sadness angered my siblings. "Why are you doing this to Mom!" They'd say, one after the other.

These reactions gave me insight into the family dynamics. It really put a spotlight on the dysfunction. This helped me to understand how things were in my house when I was growing up. The message was, "Do not be an individual!" Another implied message was to not make decisions solely for myself. I had to take everyone's feelings into account when I made a decision. That is impossible. You can't please everybody. But if I tried to think independently I was cast as a troublemaker.

When I began working at the CBOT when I was 17-years-old, I brought that dysfunctional decision making process with me. My behavior looked to others as though I really had others in my thoughts as I made a decision. Naturally this sat very well with the people I worked with. What was really going on is me trying to please everyone. I wanted to be on everyone's good side. That doesn't work. If I've learned anything in the last 13 years, it's that some people aren't going to like me, period. The result of my dysfunctional behavior was an extra burden of stress that I created for myself, because I was trying to achieve the impossible.

At first this really helped my success at the CBOT. I was the quintessential pleaser. It's ironic that the very thing that helped me to succeed was one of things that helped me become a very unhappy, stress-out person.

When I relayed the reactions of my family in therapy, a new goal became 'staying the course'. I must not give in to the families group way of thinking. Though it would be a difficult process to learn, and one that would cause many changes in my life, I needed to think for myself. I need to begin untangling the un-healthy cords that emotionally and psychologically bound me to my siblings and parents. Again, I needed to become unmeshed.

Staying the course was a foreign behavior and extremely uncomfortable. It took all my energy to not give in to their demands and rejoin the family. My Introjects were at their peak during this time, constantly barraging me with shame and guilt. The only way to defeat them was to stay the course. I did.

For the next two years I stayed away from my family - no phone calls, no letters, no family gatherings. A few months before I reentered my family I received a phone call from my mother. It was August 1993. She pretty much demanded that I come back and stop the nonsense. My response to her would lay the groundwork for another enormous step in my recovery. I told her, with no emotion, "I'll be back when I am ready." Then I hung up.

I had just faced one of the biggest bullies I would ever face in my life. That day I took a step in growing from a boy to a man. It was literally a right of passage.

In the ensuing months I found that my rage was gone. In its place was merely anger. And I could manage that. My feet became very solid underneath me. I began walking taller. By Christmas of 1993, I was ready to go back to my family under my terms.

So I started making the phone calls and as quickly as the news had traveled when I left, it traveled just as fast when I came back. When I saw my sibs and parents for the first time I was in awe at my reactions to them. I wasn't scared or fearful, nor did I try to take on any of their feelings. I was separate. I could think clearly and easily observe my feelings when they did arise. I'd recognize the feeling and move on. The feelings no longer had a chokehold on me and neither did my family.

When I recognized what had happened, I knew it would be the same with all of my relationships. I knew I would stop searching for replacement fathers at the CBOT and in my personal life. I knew I'd stop looking for others' approval.

In this chapter I have summarized the progress I made between 1991 and 1993. In the next chapter we will take a more in-depth look at the work that helped me to have this success.

Chapter 42

"Jung"

In the period between mid 1991 and Christmas 1993, a number of things took place therapeutically for me to accomplish the separation from my family, the most important being my introduction to Jungian therapy. This chapter will summarize my work.

* * *

When I separated from my family, I had to prepare for it. The whole process of preparing for something like this was new to me. I was use to just reacting to situations. Just reacting isn't always appropriate. Especially when intense emotions may be involved.

I worked with all of my counselors and they told me what to expect from my family. Their predictions were all correct. Having foreknowledge of their probable reactions was of enormous help to me.

I was also acquiring new tools from my counselors. First, they were teaching me to 'think' a situation through from beginning to end. Second, they were teaching me to 'observe' my emotional reactions when I interacted with my family members. Those two tools, and recognizing reoccurring symbols that can lead to deeper understanding, are the basics to Jungian therapy.

I'm not going to get into Jung the man or the intricacies of his therapy. You can do that yourself and you certainly don't need me to tell you my take on Jung. Read about him and draw your own conclusions. What I *will* do is focus on the two of the basic tools I mentioned above, "observing your feelings" and "think it through". Both tools were vital in my recovery, and yet it has taken years of practicing both tenets for them to be completely integrated into my life. But in 1991 I put them to work for the first time and immediately I got results.

(You may argue that my take on Jung is incorrect. That's okay. I came to my own conclusions and they worked for me.)

Here is the plan that worked for me in the process of separating myself from my family. First, I planned what I was going to say. Next I anticipated their reactions and prepared for this. This helped to desensitize myself to the reactions. This helped with my emotions. I called them individually, which disabled the possibility of having to deal with a group reaction. I let them have their reactions, but I did not get involved in their reactions. Instead I just acknowledge them. I did not get emotional with them. Instead I wrote down anything I needed to during the conversation and took any feelings I was having to group or individual therapy for discussion, or for working through.

Now I'll go into each step in more detail, so that if you need to do a separation too, you'll understand the reasoning for each one.

"Call them individually." By talking to my sibs and parents individually I took away the group mentality and stopped them from ganging up on me. Ganging up on an individual member of the family was common in our family and I needed to diffuse this. It was really bizarre when I talked to them on the phone and they wouldn't say the word, "I". Every one of them, except for my Mom, used the word, "we", as if they were speaking for everyone.

"Let them have their reactions." The first step in becoming separate from my siblings and parents was to literally let them talk about how they felt and just listen. This taught me to respect their feelings. If I wanted to interrupt them or defend myself, then I wrote it down on a piece of paper instead of butting into the middle of what they were saying. This also kept the conversation under control. There was no chance of the conversation spiraling into an argument. Finally, there was no opportunity for me to indulge in my own dysfunctional habits.

"Do not get involved in their reactions, just acknowledge them." Acknowledging someone else's feelings is powerful. Repeating back to them what they said shows you care and were paying attention. I could use this tool instead of getting hooked into a potentially dysfunctional exchange.

"Write down anything I need to during the conversation." This is a tool that helped me to get through what could have been a very emotional conversation. By writing down my feelings as they occurred during the conversation I was putting the feelings aside for the time being. I would address those feelings at a later time and in the appropriate place. This particular conversation, the notification of my intentions to separate myself from the family for a period of time, wasn't the time to express the emotional stuff that I was still working on.

"Do not get emotional with them." Emotions are the fire the brings dysfunctional relationships to a boil. If the person you have a dysfunctional relationship with is comfortable with the dysfunction, they will be expecting and perhaps even wanting those emotions. Their part of the dysfunction needs the heat. With my siblings it was a part of the dance we did during our childhood. Calmness was not the norm. We were use to mayhem. So I talked evenly and calmly. I was amazed to realize how much that helped my emotional state. After I hung up the phone with each of them I didn't feel all crazy inside. I felt as though I didn't take their emotions onto myself, as I had before.

"Take any feelings I was having to group or individual therapy and discuss those feelings." I talked about this in an earlier chapter. I just said it differently. I wrote, "…I was learning something else just as important as talking about my feelings. That was knowing *who* I should talk to about my feelings." By doing this, I was learning to tolerate carrying my feelings until I could address them appropriately. I was learning that I could have much better interpersonal relationships if I didn't let everything that came to my lips, pass them.

To really understand Jung I had to work with a Jungian therapist. It happened that one of the therapists I was working with, Barbara, was a Jungian therapist. I ended my work with Judith and Barbara became my new guide in 1992.

Judith had taken me as far as she could and it was time for me to be with someone who was similar to me, behaviorally. Judith and I were anything but. Nevertheless, I needed to be with her at the start of the process. It wouldn't have worked to be with someone similar to me in the beginning, for a thousand reasons. I was thankful for Judith's help, but it was time to move on.

Barbara was similar to me behaviorally. She studied Martial Arts (She is a Black-Belt in Chung Moo Quan), she is Irish and she has five children. I was worried that I was choosing someone like my mother for a therapist, when I decided to see Barbara, but she wasn't my mother - maybe a mother figure, but a very emotionally healthy one – a good roll model.

My therapy starting shifting from working on my feelings exclusively to incorporating the thought process. A process that I had essentially left behind since puberty.

It was foreign to think through the consequences of actions instead is simply reacting to a situation. Over and over Barbara slowly guided me through the process. The delight of working with Barbara was her similarity to Rob Ahrens, in that she allowed me to express all of my feelings. No matter how warped I perceived them to be. This aspect of our therapy became vital to my mental health. To this day I still express everything I am feeling. But I do it with the right person.

One of Barbara's techniques was to help me objectify my feelings by getting them outside of myself. If I could get them out and look at them objectively, then I could also begin to see the difference between simply reacting on an emotional level, and instead thinking my way through a situation.

I remember two ways that Barbara helped me to objectify my feelings. She had me draw them in an art book. Whatever ended up in there I'd bring to our sessions to talk them over, if I wished. We also did sand trays. Sand trays are compromised of a two-foot by one-foot box with one inch of sand in it. Barbara had hundreds of figures on shelves in her basement. The idea was to take these figures and make anything you wanted with them. I made dioramas of my feelings. Then observed them.

I saw Barbara once a week, three to four times a month over the two and half years I was away from my family. I also continued to go to group therapy once a week and see Rob about one or two times a month.

That's the basic formula I used to help me separate from my family and then to reenter it. I wish there was a magical formula I could describe here that would work for anyone. There just isn't. These are the things that worked for me. Maybe my path will generate some ideas for you or suggest a starting point for your path to mental health.

Chapter 43

"Leaving Mom's Teepee"

Rob mentioned that I should look into a men's organization called, "The Man Kind Project." Rob was a leader within that community and he said he'd stand by me of I chose to get involved. Rob was saying it was time for me to leave Momma's teepee and go live with Dad for a while. I was still a Mamma's boy and I needed to get some balance.

* * *

I deliberated with myself as I began to consider this chapter. What will people say? What will people think? What will my siblings say? My Mother? I 'm taking a big risk revealing the work I did. Maybe my co-workers will crucify me! Maybe I'll be the butt of jokes for the next ten years!

All valid concerns, and I've learned that it's a good idea to think things through before making a leap. Nevertheless, this decision was a no-brainer to me. Although on some level I need to be accepted by me peers and I perhaps risked being the butt of jokes, what I have written in this book is far more important than worrying about what others think of me. I have seen too many men in the last seven years who needed to hear that they are not alone.

Just a month ago my long-time friend Mark killed himself. I had known Mark since high school. We chose similar paths in life. Mark went to the Mercantile Exchange after high school and worked there until his death. He left brothers, sisters, a Mom and Dad, nieces and nephews and a girlfriend with two children behind. All asking themselves the question, "Why?"

I asked myself the same thing. That got me thinking about a list of what-ifs. I wondered, what if I'd approached Mark about the work I was doing? Would it have helped? What a crime that I didn't. What stopped me? The answer to that is the proverbial, "Will he laugh at me? Will he tell everyone I'm an idiot?" Deep down I know Mark would of never have done that. He was a great human being. The point is, I let my own fear get in the way. The fear of not being accepted by others. I've lived in the fear shadow for too long. It's time to allay the shadow.

* * *

I chose to see a female therapist in the beginning and that was by sub-conscious design. There was *no way* I'd have walked into a male therapists office at the beginning. I didn't trust other men and held a good deal of hostility about them within.

So I chose two female massage therapists, then Judith, but Judith pushed me into seeing Rob. She knew that I had to see a male at some point to experience compassion from an emotionally healthy man. Off to Rob I went. Just the same, meanwhile I continued to see my female massage therapists, and a female dietician.

There was one other man in my therapeutic life, the psychiatrist I saw for my anti-depressants, but my appointments with him were only 15-minutes long, and I was outta there. Plus I had Pete Garces helping me with weight training. Decidedly though, I was more comfortable with women, the point being, I needed more work with men.

My path now was the warrior community, but before I could do this, I had to say goodbye to the people I'd been working with for the last five years. I did that in early 1994 and did it with no reservations. No second thoughts or apprehensions. For the first time in my life I was making decisions with confidence and resolve.

I'm still in contact with the people who I went through those first years of intensive group therapy with. They have become an extended family of brothers and sisters. We all shared our thoughts and feeling at a time when none of us was sure of anything. We all took huge risks and leaps of faith every Thursday night hoping we'd get to some place of peace. I think we all have.

* * *

The collective experiences of our lives, both on a conscious level and on an unconscious level, form our frame of reference. In other words, our life experience, especially when we are young, molds us into who we are. I am a product of the totality of what I have experienced, including what I was taught by my teachers, peers, and my family members. Our frame of reference is not an immutable thing. When we are willing to be open-minded, to seek new experiences, new teachers and new peers, we began to change. We change from the inside out. Our frame of reference changes.

I think the term plays a very important role when addressing the issues I had with men. There is no other man in my life that had a bigger impact on man-to-man relationships than my Father. I sought other males out during my life that were similar in behavior to my Father. I dealt with men in society as my father dealt with men. This not only reinforced the messages my

Dad sent me, it was also a way to prove to myself that my dad was a good father, that he was 'right'. I built my internal parent based on his parenting.

When I realized that my father's way of parenting was not working for me any more, I needed to seek a different way to parent myself. That's what Rob was trying to get across. So, I started moving into a men's community that had been built up in the Chicago area. What I found within that community of men was nothing less than astonishing.

* * *

My first encounter with this community of men was on a weekend in September of 1994. I can't write about the specifics of what happened that weekend due to confidentiality, but I can say this. The effect on me was profound. If you are a man who has been searching for something in your life. If something has been missing throughout your life, then you can fulfill a great deal of that emptiness by participating with a healthy community of men. Please don't be afraid because I won't reveal what happened that weekend. I wouldn't put you in harms way. This group is anything but harmful. It's not a religious organization. It's not a cult. Look in the back of this book for more information about this phenomenal community of men.

What was provided to me on that initial weekend has also changed the lives of thousands and thousands of men throughout the world. What happens is so powerful that chapters have been created in many different States and Countries.

When I had completed that weekend in September of 1994, I had truly left my mothers teepee. I had moved to my father's teepee, and was well on my way to developing into a healthy man.

After that weekend I joined up with a new group. This one was not a therapy group. It was compromised of eight men who had been on the same weekend journey. We'd come together once a week for two or three hours to talk and resolve the problems we were having in the present. The results were astounding. The men in that group began achieving things in their lives they never thought possible. From reconciled marriages to resolutions with their parents. Many went on to begin new exciting careers because they had broken down so many barriers of fear that had built up inside them. And the list of accomplishments goes on and on.

I *can* talk about what I worked on within this community without breaking any confidences. I worked on my relationships with men and more specifically, with my father. I talked with other men about my relationship with my father in the present and the past. I did what is called, "Going down to the ashes", the place within me that is in the muck, the bottom of the well so to speak. This is the place where all of the hurtful, painful feelings reside in our soul. Here resided the *real* thoughts and feelings I had about my Dad. I had peeled the onion so far down in the last five years I was able to get to that place. I was able to reveal my inner-most feelings having to do with my father. There was no drugs or alcohol in my system to cover the hate, anger and raw fear I had about my Dad. These things had to be confronted - and I was ready. What I found in the ashes were years of pent-up rage, anger and fear. During that weekend I raged about him and the ways he treated me through my life. I raged at his lack of emotions and about his constant drinking. I raged about my father's complete ignorance of the intense feels that bounced around my soul every minute of every day. I had no clue what they were. I needed guidance. I needed compassion. I received none of this! My father was an absent father. He provided monetarily and that was it. I needed more. Much, much more.

When puberty hit, it was all out chaos within myself. Puberty was the time I needed my father the most and that is when he failed me the most. I raged and raged. Finally I revealed that my father went to my mother and said that he couldn't handle me. After that, she would have to be responsible for raising me the rest of the way. No wonder I was a mamma's boy!

When I confronted these emotions in this supportive group of compassionate men, suddenly I realized that there was no internal confusion anymore. There were no inner voices telling me that I should be ashamed of myself for doing this, or telling me to be grateful for what I have and shut up. Those voices were gone. There was no guilt. Instead, I had taken a big chance and was rewarded with a new model of what it is to be a man among men. I found another kind of man, a kind that is supportive and compassionate, as well as strong.

For a year I worked with this men's community. I worked my issues and in September of 1995 started to come to resolve. The road that lay ahead emerged into something different and glorious. This was the last leg of the journey. I was entering a place of peace, resolution and something I never expected - *gratefulness* for my father.

Chapter 44

"My Father"

Peter C. Goulding, Jr., died on the September 3rd, 1998. I spent the prior three years trying to talk with him, trying to come to some agreement with him, trying to be friends.

He was the dedicated father of six children. He was Grandfather to thirteen children, Great-grandfather to one. He was a husband, to Mary, for forty-seven-years, until his death.

He was a man who had an effect on *everyone's* life in the United States. He's the man who championed the implementation of fluoridated water in the 1960's for the American Dental Association (ADA). He worked at the ADA his whole life and received numerous awards throughout his career, including; the Citation of Merit Award from the American College of Dentists and the Greater New York Academy of Prosthodontics Achievement Award. He was well published in Dental and medical journals and national magazines.

He served in numerous organizations like, the Public Relations Society of America, the National Association of Science Writers and the American Association for the Advancements of Sciences.

He spoke at hundreds of dental society meetings both nationally and internationally and was the central figure in the development of the ADA Public Education Program. He was an honorary member of the American Dental Society of Anesthesiology.

Earlier in his life he was a radio operator for the Navy during WWII, in the Philippines. After the war he went to DePaul University and graduated third in his class.

My father grew up poor, in the inner city of Chicago. He had one brother and one sister. His Father, Peter Sr., came to America on the ship the Philadelphia on September 6th, 1916, alone and just seventeen-years-old. He was looking for the streets of gold like so many of his fellow Irish countrymen were. He did not find that elusive dream. What he found was a life of hardship. A life of menial jobs and endless worry.

My Grandfather was from Galway, Ireland. In 1995 I went to Ireland to visit my family's roots. Both my parents had family from Ireland. We made a stop in Cohb, Ireland to see a museum that had been built for the ocean liner the Titanic, because that's the last port of call the Titanic sailed from. What I found there, in Cohb, was bigger than the Titanic. What I saw there would forever change my life.

When I visited the exhibit commemorating the Titanic, I noticed another exhibit there. It was an extensive presentation about the emigration that took place from Ireland to the U.S., just after the potato famine.

There was thorough documentation about what it was like for the Irish people who traveled aboard the ships to America, what the conditions were like on the ships and what they faced when they got to America. One mans anonymous quote put it all together. He said, "We all came looking for streets of gold and only found more poverty. After working for years in America and realizing 99.9% of us would never get rich in America there was only one dream we could foster. That dream is that our children and their children would have a better life than we did".

I am a descendant of that dream.

After WWII my Father saw an opportunity and jumped on it. That opportunity came via the GI Bill. He was able to attend DePaul University. However, the opportunity to go to DePaul really was not created by the U.S. Navy's G.I. Bill program. My Grandfather created that opportunity. My dad was realizing the benefits of being a citizen of the U.S. He seized those benefits so his children would not have to grow up poor as he did in the streets of Chicago. His children would have a big house, a closet full of clothes, a garage full of bikes, food on the table and money in the bank if they wanted to go to college. He would pay for all the expenses that went with college so they didn't have to work side jobs as he had, when he went to DePaul University in Chicago.

I had great success at The Chicago Board of trade at a very young age. The Chicago Board of Trade did not provide that success though. My Grandfathers, Grandmothers, my Mother and my Father provided it for me.

For the first time in my life I became very grateful for what my ancestors and more specifically my parents had done for me. All that I have in this world is due to so many others' sacrifices, especially my parents.

I couldn't have gotten to this place of gratitude had I not entered the pit of my fears and demon's. There was no bypass to this place. I had to go directly through it to emerge with hope and inner peace. I had to face those inner demon's that had once barraged my brain with endless contradicting statements, feelings and thoughts. I had to peal the onion one layer at a time and constantly take leaps of faith. I had to feel my way around a whole new universe of emotions and thoughts as if I had been blinded. To get to the place of hope and peace I had to blame others, speak my truth, yell, rage, cry and trust.

* * *

In the last year of Dad's life he faced escalating deterioration of his mind and body. He was never a physically healthy man. Beginning with his first bout of tuberculosis in 1952 to his second bout with it in 1960 when he had half his lung removed. In the late 1960's he was diagnosed with rheumatoid arthritis. The disease ravaged his body in the cruelest ways, eventually taking all his bones in his knuckles and knees. All were replaced surgically and seemed to extend his life. To combat the pain of this ugly debilitating disease, he drank alcohol. As his Father did.

He drank every day starting at lunch and then continuing when he got home from work until he went to bed. Because of his constant drinking he became numbed and passive in my life.

I was the last of six children. By the time I came along, in December of 1961, my Dad was still healing from the removal of his lower right lung, a year and a half prior. The oldest child in our family was eight. Both my parents had their hands full with six children between the ages of newborn and eight. By the time I was ten, the onset of rheumatoid arthritis began and my Dad's health dropped quickly over the next five years.

Despite the sicknesses my Father suffered, he got up and went to work everyday. No complaints. I never heard one pass his lips. My Dad did the best he could with what was given to him. He surpassed his brother and sister in academics and determination so he'd make something of himself in the working world and provide for his family. I was lucky to be his son and he was lucky to have a son like me.

Chapter 45

"September 7th 1995"

The Chicago Board of Trade became less and less important to me from 1993 through 1995. The more therapy I did and Martial Arts I studied, the less important money and notoriety were in my life. I left Bob Lasers trading operation in 1993 and traded as a local for a year before joining another trading operation.

I was really working part-time over those last two years at the CBOT. I had nothing left to give the trading pit. I'd been lucky enough to save a considerable amount of money. What that money afforded me was the time and capital to invest in healing.

Finally I did reach my goal of mental and physical health. The time had come for goodbyes.

In August 1995, I said goodbye to Barbara and Jungian therapy, then said goodbye to the group of men I'd been working with for the last year. Finally, I said goodbye to Rob Ahrens.

On September 7th, 1995, exactly sixteen-years to the day, I said goodbye to the Chicago Board of Trade. My heart was no longer in it.

Chapter 46

"Conclusion"

This book is about a search for a relationship with my father. Although I never got the conversation I dreamed about with him, I did come to a place of peace within myself about that relationship.

The search began in 1979 as I entered the CBOT and sought out father figures in the work place. Every time the search failed I drove deeper and deeper into the world of money, drugs and alcohol to alleviate the painful need inside of me. Somehow, I thought that the pain would stop if I had just one more drink, took one more drug or made another million. When that didn't work, I turned to therapy in early 1988. By the end of 1995, I had found what I was looking for.

This book is about sharing my experiences in hope that you may draw parallels. In hope that you may choose to take control of your life. Your path may not look similar to mine, nor will it be. But there is one thing that is common about our roads – the commonality of feelings. If you want to get to a place of inner peace you will have to confront your feelings. I hope that I have given you a glimpse of what that confrontation looks like. I hope that I have given you the courage to take the first leap of faith to reach out and ask for help.

This book is about the effects of things we have no control over and about the things we can take control of. It's about choices in life, my choices and no one else's. It's about owning my behaviors and actions. It's about blaming others to get to a place of blamelessness. It's about knowing that there are other ways to live and there are people out there who will help you get there. You just have to hold on tight and take that leap of faith.

End

Afterword

On October 9, 2001, I walked back into the Bond Pit in the Chicago Board of Trade. It had been just over six-years since I had walked out of the CBOT for good. I was so convinced I would never walk back into the CBOT again; I sold the second and last of the two memberships I owned in April 2001. I had given up on the CBOT and put it into my rearview mirror. That's until I got a call from Bill Erdmier. (You'll notice his name in the beginning of the book under the 'Thank You' section.)

I didn't think there was a human being who could ever convince me to re-enter the Board. I had sincerely thought it was behind me and I was going to continue moving forward. But Billy convinced me. This time it was a friend guiding me and not a father figure. That's a solid reassurance to me. It tells me how far I've come. It also tells me that I have a very close friend in Bill. I'm very lucky for that friendship.

To move forward I had to go backwards. Go figure? My return to the CBOT wasn't close to what I expected it to be. I was greeted with open arms and smiling faces. People were genuinely concerned how I was, where I had been and how my family was. Those reactions brought me out of a three-year struggle. A three-year struggle trying to find out where I belonged in the work world. After my first day back, I realized I had come full circle and knew instantly where I belonged. You could of put a gun to my head a year ago and I wouldn't have walked back into the Board. I wasn't ready.

Therapy is a great tool. A tool that shouldn't be discarded once you start the process. As of this writing I am completing another round of therapy. I may stop shortly and take some time off until I need it again. By far, these last few months have been the greatest for me since I began therapy in 1989. I can think clearer than ever before. I can tolerate my feelings better.

I am still clean and sober and will celebrate my eleventh year this New Years Eve. Diana and I are stronger than ever. We celebrated our 18th wedding anniversary this year. I am an extremely lucky man. Diana has been with me since the beginning and we'll be together at the end. I'm so blessed to be married to her. Our daughter, Haley Dara, is almost five and the light of our lives. I am here to guide her. She is here to guide me also.

When I left the CBOT in Sep. of 1995 I pursued becoming a teacher in Martial Arts. I had been studying for four years by then and sincerely loved every work-out at the Degerberg Academy. I became quite proficient in Kali and other forms of Philippine Martial Arts.

Furthermore, I studied Bruce Lees' "Jeet-Kun-Do", with great passion, adopting, 'No way is the way'. I was lucky enough to have been tutored by Bruce Lee's right-hand-man, Dan Inasanto himself. Not to mention, Grand Master Silute, 8nd degree Black-Belt Fred Degerberg, 2nd Degree Black-Belt Oscar Bravo and 1st Degree Black-Belt Mike Whitman. My dream of Black-Belt died in late 1996 due to a severe back injury while sparing. I was *this* close to it. In one day it was over. Although I continue to pursue, practice and study Martial Arts, my heavy training days are over due to that injury.

I started a business in 1996 and sold it in 1999. Then became a coach/consultant to people struggling in the industry I came from, the financial industry. I also became a certified behavior analyst to help corporations teach their employees to communicate with each other by understanding their own behaviors first. These two things I'm passionate about. Feel free to visit my web site, www.imacoach.com. Oh yea, I also became an author. Who'd a thunk that fifteen years ago?

I sincerely hope that you, the reader, benefited from my tale. If there were a few nuggets you took from the book, then I have done my job. If you make that phone call for help, even better. Most importantly, I wanted to get across that I am just a common man. Nothing separates you and I. If I can get clean and sober, I know you can too.

Know that you are not alone. Know that you have options. Yes, some are harder than others. But in the end, you'll choose the correct path and I really am cheering you on. Know that the time I spent in therapy worked. I am a completely different human being now, thanks to the many phenomenal people who helped me over my journey.

Feel free to email me anytime if I can be of service to you. No question is too silly. Just write to: jamesg4@yahoo.com.

Take care,
Jim
November 3rd, 2001.

Pink Floyd Main Members past and present:
Syd Barret, Roger Water, Dave Gilmour, Rick Wright, Nick Mason.

Lyrics in this book are almost all written by Roger Waters with some written by David Gilmour and Bob Ezrin.

My Pink Floyd recommended CD's;
**Dark Side of The Moon
*Animals
**The Wall
Momentary Lapse of Reason
Division Bell
*Any of the live CD sets

Rush Members:
Geddy Lee, Neil Peart, Alex Lifeson.
My Rush recommended CD's;
Rush (Self Titled)
Fly By Night
Caress of Steel
**2112
**All the Worlds a Stage(Live)
*A Farewell to Kings
**Hemispheres
**Permanent Waves
**Moving Pictures
**Exit Stage Left
Counterparts
**Different Stages (Live)

*Favorites
** Must have

SELF-HELP RESOURCES

Alcoholics Anonymous
AA's Home Page.
http://www.alcoholics-anonymous.org/

Narcotics Anonymous
Narcotics Anonymous Home Page.
http://www.na.org/

Therapy
If you live in the Chicago are, here are some excellent therapists that I personally worked with during my recovery. You couldn't be in better hands.
Rob Ahrens, Licensed Clinical Social Worker, President, Conscious Health Initiative, Inc., Evanston Illinois, 847-609-7174.
Dave Lingren, Conscious Health Initiative, Inc. Evanston Illinois, 847-609-7174.

If you are not from the Chicago area please visit this excellent web site to help you find a therapist.
http://www.1-800-therapist.com/index.html

Massage Therapy
American Massage Therapy Association Home Page. A great site for assisting you in finding a certified AMTA Massage Therapist.
http://www.amtamassage.org
The Rolf Institute of Structural Integration Home Page.
http://www.rolf.org/

Quotes

Chapter 1
CD: "Dark Side of the Moon"
Song: Breathe
Music Water/Gilmour/Wright
Lyrics: Waters
Produced by Pink Floyd
Harvest/EMI/Capitol/Columbia/MFSL

Chapter 2
CD: "Animals"
Song: Dogs
Music: Waters/Gilmour
Lyrics: Waters
Produced by Pink Floyd
Harvest/EMI/Columbia

Chapter 3
CD: "Wish You Were Here"
Song: Wish You Were Here
Music: Waters/Gilmour
Lyrics: Waters
Produced by Pink Floyd
Harvest/Columbia/EMI

Chapter 4
CD: 2112
Song: 2112 (Part III. Discovery)
Music by Rush
Lyrics: Peart
Anthem/Mercury/Poly Gram

Chapter 5
CD: Moving Pictures
Song: Red Barchetta
Music by Rush
Lyrics: Peart
Anthem/Mercury/Poly Gram

Chapter 6
CD: A Farewell To Kings
Song: Xanadu
Music by Rush
Lyrics: Peart
Anthem/Mercury/Poly Gram Records

Chapter 7
CD: 2112
Song: 2112 (Part VI. Soliloquy)
Music by Rush
Lyrics: Peart
Anthem/Mercury/Poly Gram

Chapter 8
CD: "Wish You Were Here"
Song: Have a Cigar
Music: Roger Waters
Lyrics: Roger Waters
Produced by Pink Floyd
Harvest/Columbia/EMI

Chapter 9
CD: "Wish You Were Here"
Song: Have a Cigar
Music: Waters
Lyrics: Waters
Produced by Pink Floyd
Harvest/Columbia/EMI

Chapter 10
CD: "The Wall"
Song: The Thin Ice
Music: Waters
Lyrics: Roger Waters
Produced by Pink Floyd
Harvest/EMI/Columbia

Chapter 11
CD: "The Wall"
Song: Comfortably Numb
Music: Gilmour/Waters
Lyrics: Waters
Produced by Pink Floyd
Harvest/EMI/Columbia

Chapter 12
CD: "The Wall"
Song: The Trial
Music: Waters/Ezrin
Lyrics: Waters
Produced by Pink Floyd
Harvest/EMI/Columbia

Chapter 13
CD: "The Wall"
Song: The Thin Ice
Music: Waters
Lyrics: Waters
Produced by Pink Floyd
Harvest/EMI/Columbia

Chapter 14
CD: 2112
Song: Something For Nothing
Music by Rush
Lyrics: Peart
Anthem/Mercury/Poly Gram

Chapter 15
CD: Permanent Waves
Song: Natural Science
Music by Rush
Lyrics: Peart
Anthem/Mercury/Poly Gram

Chapter 16
CD: Permanent Waves
Song: Jacob's Ladder
Music by Rush
Lyrics: Peart
Anthem/Mercury/Poly Gram

Chapter 17
CD: Counterparts
Song: Nobody's Hero
Music by Rush
Lyrics: Peart
Anthem/Atlantic

Chapter 18
CD: "A Momentary Lapse of Reason"
Song: Learning to Fly
Music: Gilmour/Exrin/Moore/

Carin
Produced by: Bob Ezrin
and David Gilmour
EMI/Columbia

Chapter 19
CD: Counterparts
Song: Animate
Music by Rush
Lyrics: Peart
Anthem/Atlantic

Chapter 20
CD: 2112
Song: 2112 (Part II.
Temples of Syrinx)
Music by Rush
Lyrics: Peart
Anthem/Mercury/
Poly Gram

Chapter 21
CD: "Dark Side of the Moon"
Song: Money
Music Waters
Lyrics: Waters
Produced by Pink Floyd
Harvest/EMI/Capitol/
Columbia/MFSL

Chapter 22
CD: A Farewell To Kings
Song: Cynus X-1, Book One: The Voyage
Music by Rush
Lyrics: Peart
Anthem/Mercury/
Poly Gram Records

Chapter 23
CD: A Farewell To Kings
Song: Cinderella Man
Music by Rush
Lyrics: Peart
Anthem/Mercury/
Poly Gram Records

Chapter 24
CD: A Farewell To Kings
Song: Madrigal Man
Music by Rush
Lyrics: Peart
Anthem/Mercury/
Poly Gram Records

Chapter 25
Chapter 1
CD: "Dark Side of the Moon"
Song: Eclipse
Music Water
Lyrics: Waters
Produced by Pink Floyd
Harvest/EMI/Capitol/
Columbia/MFSL

Opening quote in "Part I"
"Dying is easy, it's living that scares me to death"
CD: Diva
Lyrics: Annie Lenox
Song: Cold
Arista Records, BMG
Ariola Munchen Gmbh.

About the Author

Jim Goulding is a commodity trader at the Chicago Board of Trade in Chicago, IL. He's 39-years-old. He lives in Elmhurst, IL., with his wife Diana and their daughter Haley Dara. Jim and Diana have been married for 18 years. Haley is 5-years-old.